TELLING
RIGHT
FROM
WRONG

TELLING RIGHT FROM WRONG

WHAT IS MORAL, WHAT IS IMMORAL, AND WHAT IS NEITHER ONE NOR THE OTHER

by
Timothy J. Cooney

Prometheus Books
700 E. AMHERST ST. BUFFALO, NEW YORK 14215

Published 1985 by Prometheus Books
700 East Amherst Street, Buffalo, New York 14215

Copyright © 1985 by Timothy J. Cooney
All Rights Reserved

Library Of Congress Card Number: 85-61123
ISBN 0-87975-297-1

Printed in the United States of America

To Beth Preddy

Contents

Acknowledgments

There is an Afterword to this book in which I explain some of the peculiar circumstances surrounding its publication (it was originally set for publication by Random House). In the Afterword my debts to a number of people will become clear, but let me at this point mention several people who were very helpful to me: Laura Schultz and Becky Saletan, editorial assistants at Random House, who made the book better; Laurie Stearns, my copy editor at Random House, who made many of the sentences clearer; Allisyn René Gras, an adviser, critic and friend; Wendy Jones, who helped with some of the earlier copyediting; Peggy Kirby and Judy Strom who offered valuable suggestions; N. Shaam Krasner, with whom I walked the streets of our beloved phantasmagoria and talked the craft of writing, of which he is an expert; and my neighbors, Mary Kay Bullard and Joseph Cronin, who carried the burden of my frustrations with charm and grace. To say that there would not have been a book without the help of these people is to say the obvious. The defects of my work are, of course, my own responsibility.

Manhattan
February 1985

Publisher's Note

Timothy J. Cooney's book *Telling Right From Wrong* has provoked enormous controversy. Even before it was scheduled for publication, some argued that it should never be printed and that, if it were published, it should be boycotted.

The facts of the Cooney affair, now a cause celebrè, are as follows: Timothy Cooney is not a professional philosopher, though he has an avid interest in moral questions. He had previously written two other books but was unable to find a publisher for them. He encountered the same difficulty with the manuscript of *Telling Right From Wrong.*

In this book, Cooney wrestles with some of the most difficult questions of twentieth-century moral philosophy: What is morality? How should the terms "moral" and "immoral" be used? He has developed his own unique and innovative theory for delineating the issues involved.

Unfortunately, Cooney was unable to get even a reading of his manuscript. Trade publishers generally avoid philosophical and moral issues, and university presses often refuse to consider manuscripts by authors who lack the requisite academic credentials. Acting out of desperation and in the hope of gaining entrance to the publishing world, Cooney wrote a letter extolling the virtues of his manuscript and signed the name of Robert Nozick, a well-known American philosopher.

Prior to this forgery, however, and quite independent of it, an editor at Random House expressed interest in seeing the manuscript on the basis of reading the introduction and an outline of the book, which Cooney had submitted. The editor had heard of the endorsement and requested to see it as well. Cooney then forwarded the remainder of his manuscript accompanied by the falsified letter. Soon thereafter a contract was issued and the process of publication began. However, the editor eventually learned the facts of the forgery, and Random House decided to withdraw publication of the book.

Although we at Prometheus understand Mr. Cooney's desire to obtain a hearing for his manuscript, we consider his behavior inexcusable. Moreover, we agree with the decision of Random House not to go forward with publication, for Mr. Cooney had misrepresented his book by submitting a fraudulent endorsement.

Following the storm of publicity created by his deception and by the Random House reaction, Mr. Cooney sent his manuscript of *Telling Right From Wrong* to Prometheus for consideration. We decided to undertake publication for the following reasons:

The central issue was the relative merit of the work itself. Was it worthy of publication, notwithstanding the moral transgressions of the author? Our answer to that question was yes. We firmly believe that *Telling Right From Wrong* is an original, if not brilliant, contribution to the field of moral philosophy. Mr. Cooney's lack of academic credentials and/or the fact that he holds no teaching position is quite irrelevant to the issue of publication. Many distinguished authors of philosophy—such as Spinoza, Schopenhauer, Kierkegaard, Nietzsche, Marx, John Stuart Mill, and even Charles S. Pierce—had few formal credentials, held no academic posts, or were rejected by the academic philosophers of their day.

In publishing *Telling Right From Wrong*, Prometheus does not agree or disagree with the author's thesis; rather, we believe that the book deserves to be judged on its own merits. We deplore any suggestion that it should be permanently censured or banned because of an unconscionable act of its author. Such a criterion would only serve to decimate the literary landscape.

Although *Telling Right From Wrong* is a plea for tolerance concerning many moral questions, it is well to note that Mr.

Cooney himself has not sought to defend his act of forgery. In his Afterword, he has applied his strongest indictment to this kind of behavior.

No doubt it will be perplexing to the reader to learn that an author who writes so eloquently on moral philosophy should violate his own principles. In spite of this, we firmly believe that *Telling Right From Wrong* is an insightful, thought-provoking, and controversial book that deserves to be published.

Paul Kurtz
Editor and Publisher

Introduction

Today there seems to be growing discomfort, if not embarrassment, with the question of morality. Morality has always had a dark side, the killing and punishing of the immoral in fits of moral rectitude; tell us that "Smith is a very moral man," and we are not at all sure we want to be involved with him. "Moralist" is often a pejorative term, and the word "morality" itself seems to be slipping in that direction. Yet the words "right" and "wrong" seem as healthy and as traditionally used as ever, though, if pressed, the speaker often acknowledges that he or she means morally right, or morally wrong, at which point the listener may disagree and the next moment tempers flare. We step in to try to calm things down but don't succeed, and indeed we may get angry ourselves, for at the heart of the problem there is this unanswered question: "What is morality?"

In a narrow sense it is not too difficult to find the answer. When we go to the common usage of the word "morality"—when we listen carefully to how the word is used and note how it is not used in ordinary discourse—we find that a quite precise definition of the word itself emerges, namely, an ultimate and universal guide to action. It would sound odd for a believer in God to say, "This act is immoral: it is contrary to the word of God, but even more important. . . ." For the believer there is nothing more important than the word of God; His word is morality, the ultimate guide to action.* It would sound equally odd for a believer to say, "This act

---

*The concept of an ultimate guide does not necessarily mean a guide to *all* action. Indeed, historically, it never has. Even the most devoutly religious individuals

is contrary to the word of God and is immoral for *some* people to do." In short, while morality is the word of God for a believer, it is also, by the definition we uncover, an ultimate and universal guide to action.

But when we listen to nonbelievers use the word, this same definition of morality emerges. It would sound odd for anyone to say, "This is immoral, but even more important . . ." or "Abortion is a basic *moral right* for *some* women." (Again the sense of ultimateness and universality.) However, because a word has a precise definition does not guarantee that it represents anything in the real world (e.g., the word "unicorn" has a precise definition). This brings us to the deeper meaning of the question "What is morality?"—namely, does it actually exist? Is there an ultimate and universal guide to action? Or, to put the question another way: If God does not exist, or if, in any case, He never spoke to man, what then, *if anything*, is the foundation for ethical knowledge and for the list of "dos and don'ts" (Thou shalt not kill, etc.) that we are all familiar with and that have passed for moral truth for centuries?

For the approximately eighty years between the publication of John Stuart Mill's *Utilitarianism* and the beginning of World War II, this deeper question was probably the single most important problem in Western philosophy. And for one of those rare times in the history of philosophy, philosophers felt a considerable urgency to their work, for it was widely assumed that if they (or someone) did not come up with a new foundation for the traditional list of dos and don'ts, knowable to, and accepted by, most rational men and women, then—as the masses caught up with the intellectuals' disbelief in a talking God—anarchy would be loosed upon the world, and everyone would do whatever he or she wanted.† Nor did the urgency lessen as disbeliefs spread and

---

have usually recognized areas of life where their ultimate guide doesn't guide—for example, the cloistered monk may have a free choice as to how he wants his eggs—which is to say that we can have an ultimate guide that covers only certain acts, which is further to say that there are areas of life not covered by morality.

†If the guide was not generally accepted and if there were many guides around, pointing to opposite conclusions on specific acts, then we would also end up with anarchy. The prevailing assumption was that anarchy was something to be

writers and poets came to write endlessly of their despair in a world without values and moral authority—a wasteland of hollow men, strangers, dead souls, and outsiders.

Hard pressed, philosophers came up with solutions to the problem of morality without God, only to have them knocked down by other philosophers. (Every solution seemed to fall quickly before the *metaethical* question "How do you know you have chosen the right ultimate guide?" or "By what criterion have you chosen your criterion?") A growing consensus emerged as to what morality was not, but there was no agreement as to what it was—a point that G. E. Moore makes in *Ethics*,† and that, as we shall see, was particularly true in his case, where his "negative argument" against utilitarianism was and still is widely accepted, but his "positive argument" (what morality is) was and is generally rejected.

The growing despair that one might expect in the field reached bottom when the Logical Positivists boldly said what everyone feared: It was all a nonsense search, for morality is without rational foundation; "Stealing is wrong" simply means the speaker disapproves of stealing,‡ and the statement, despite its objective grammatical form, is not objective, verifiable, or true. Indeed, as if they had a need to make the rubble bounce, the Logical Positivists said such statements were nonsensical.

The fear was now out in the open and discussed by a lost gener-

---

avoided, but even if we don't make this assumption, we are led to the question "Is anarchy good or bad?" which gets us right back to the question "What is morality?" (What is good, what is bad?)

† London: Oxford University Press, 1912, pp. 7-8.

‡ "The presence of an ethical symbol in a proposition adds nothing to its factual content. Thus if I say to someone, 'You acted wrongly in stealing that money,' I am not stating anything more than if I had simply said, 'You stole that money.' In adding that this action is wrong I am not making any further statement about it. I am simply evincing my moral disapproval of it. It is as if I had said, 'You stole that money,' in a peculiar tone of horror, or written it with the addition of some special exclamation marks. The tone, or the exclamation marks, adds nothing to the literal meaning of the sentence. It merely serves to show that the expression of it is attended by certain feelings in the speaker." A. J. Ayer, *Language, Truth and Logic* (London: Gollancz, 1936; New York: Dover, 1946) p. 107.

ation as it asked, "Where are the values?" and replied to its own question, "There aren't any." But nothing happened—the lost generation graduated and went to work as had its parents; life went on. In time some of the most prominent philosophers, including Bertrand Russell and Ludwig Wittgenstein (perhaps a bit embarrassed for philosophy and for the assumption that if philosophers didn't come up with an answer everything would fall apart), declared the question of morality insoluble, if not meaningless and nonsensical. Even Moore, who unlike Russell and Wittgenstein had devoted a great part of his professional life to the question of morality, was reduced to despair, as we shall see.

In the end—the end of this period of intense interest by philosophers in the problem of morality—the question all but died, if not of exhaustion, then of boredom on the part of philosophers as well as almost everyone else. For over a quarter of a century (say, until the early 1970s) one can think of hardly any books or articles on morality (in any fundamental sense) that approached the earlier works in excitement or controversy. But if the subject of morality was an embarrassment for philosophers, and if the word has fallen into disuse in some circles, the words "right" and "wrong" are, as I have noted, as widely used as ever. Indeed, the word "right" or "rights" has been adopted by the new generation of philosophers that has revived interest in moral philosophy—which includes John Rawls, Robert Nozick, and Ronald Dworkin—when they talk about some of the traditional questions ('What is right?" "What is wrong?"). These philosophers try to escape the seemingly hopeless morass that earlier philosophers had found themselves in by first stating that some rights are absolute and fundamental and then examining the implications of this claim. But as much as I, and no doubt many others, may appreciate this boldness in reviving the traditional questions without worrying about the metaethical problems of old, and as noble-sounding as these rights may be,* I am

---

*"Justice is the first virtue of social institutions as truth is to thought. . . . Each person possesses an inviolability founded on justice that even the welfare of society as a whole cannot over-ride. . . . The rights secured by justice are not subject to political bargaining or to the calculus of social interests." John Rawls, A *Theory of Justice* (Cambridge: Harvard University Press, 1971), p. 3.

compelled to reach the conclusion that their firm avowal of absolute and fundamental rights is a hopelessly relativistic position,
since there is no way we can *rationally* prefer it to any other. Saying
a right is "absolute" and "fundamental" does not make it so.

I believe that there is an objective answer to the question
"What is morality?" that it is quite precise, and that the philosophers who struggled during the period I spoke of were close to it
before the question was dropped. Everyone had a piece of the
answer—George Santayana said that morality is politics; R. B.
Perry claimed that it is value, and gave a precise definition to the
term; H. D. Aiken urged that it is common interests; A. J. Ayer
thought that it is emotion; and even Moore—who said it cannot be
any *thing*, natural, supernatural, psychological, or one's desires, and
who seemed to be contradicting the basic assumption of everyone
else—also had a piece of the answer.

The trouble was that everyone was making what I will call the
great error of moral philosophy: The reason the pieces could not
be put together in a coherent whole (and pieces that didn't belong
in the design tossed out) is that everyone was starting from the
same false assumption—the great error—and only when this mistake is recognized can the riddle of morality be solved. The great
error is the failure to recognize that two substantively different matters pass under the heading of morality.

But the great error made by philosophers has been nothing less
than a tragic mistake when repeated by ordinary men and women
in the day-to-day practice of their moral beliefs. For it is here that
the fury of moral rectitude has been unleashed, the killing and punishing of so many in the name of right—even though we don't
know what right means. And it is here that solving the ancient riddle of morality may prove to be of more than academic interest.

Before closing this introduction, let me offer a rough map of
the arguments to follow: a guide that may prove helpful, especially
since I have been forced (to prove some of my points) to take
some rather long detours (and forced also to postpone a number of
my arguments until "further on," a phrase found too often in this
book, but made necessary by the fact that so many of my arguments raise more questions than I can immediately answer).

A point vital to the understanding of this book is that when I talk about language and the meaning of certain words I am—with a few exceptions—talking about them *as they occur in decision-making situations that involve two or more individuals*. In particular, I concentrate on sentences that contain the words "right" and "wrong," "good" and "bad" as they are found in both moral and nonmoral, decision-making situations.*

These words are found frequently not only in moral discourse ("Stealing is wrong") but in nonmoral discourse as well ("He's the wrong person for the job;" "It's a bad day for a picnic"). But to state the obvious, there is considerable confusion about the meaning of these words in moral discourse; and while philosophers have worked prodigiously trying to find their meanings, or to show that they have many meanings or are meaningless (in morality), philosophers are, as I have noted, no closer to agreement than they ever were. What may not seem obvious is that we often don't know what these words mean in nonmoral discourse either (e.g., when one business person says to another, "Jones is the wrong person for the job; we ought not to hire him").

I am going to argue that the logical structure of nonmoral discourse is all-but-identical to that of moral discourse. I also argue that the words "right" and "wrong," "good" and "bad" have *precise definitions* in both moral and nonmoral discourse; that the definitions of these words are *identical* in both areas; that we often use these words according to their precise definitions and get a lot of work accomplished with them; that, however, we often use these words incorrectly—and I mean by this not "grammatically in-

---

*The difference between moral and nonmoral issues is by no means generally agreed upon; indeed, getting at this distinction is central to the purpose of this book. But for now, let moral issues be those that are commonly considered as such: murder, robbery, abortion, capital punishment, and so forth. And let nonmoral issues be those that most people don't regard as moral: how to reach harbor safely, whether or not our company needs another accountant, what play to send into the football huddle. One other point: Some moralists—in particular some theologians—have argued that not only acts but thoughts can be immoral, as in "Thou shalt not covet thy neighbor's wife." They also consider some acts that don't involve others (e.g., suicide, masturbation, gluttony) to be immoral. But for the most part I think it is fair to say that morality is about decisions and acts that involve more than one person.

correct," but incorrect in a way that may cause confusion and incite anger unintentionally; that correct and incorrect usage are both so common that we have lost sight of the precise definitions, don't know what we are talking about much of the time, are confused, and are often infuriated by what we don't know and don't understand. I argue that how we talk affects how we think and act; that if we talked differently, we would think and act differently; and that while it may appear that we are trapped in a vicious circle, there is a cure—and I will offer it.

I begin by examining the basic words ("right," "wrong," etc.) as they are used in nonmoral discourse. I try to show that in this area what is said (e.g., "Jones is the wrong man for the job.") is often said because of a desire that the speaker and the listener(s) share—to make a profit, to keep their jobs, to be respected—and that satisfying this shared desire requires working and talking together and making correct decisions.

In these kinds of nonmoral, decision-making situations we often employ a rapid-fire shorthand. This shorthand leaves a lot unsaid—but when it is used correctly, what is unsaid doesn't have to be said; the listener "senses" the truth of the spoken words, the right decision is made, and the shared desire is satisfied. What is unsaid I call the *background argument*—and I try to show that even though statements using the shorthand are used countless times each day to get work done, we are only, at best, vaguely aware of this extremely complex background argument, or its nature. Thus if I give you some information about Jones (perhaps in no more than two or three words), you may say, "He's the wrong person for the job," and everyone in the room may agree with you, and we move on quickly to the next candidate. The entire discussion of Jones may have taken fifteen seconds and not raised the slightest problem for any of us. Yet if someone were to ask what is meant by "wrong person for the job"—which in effect requires us to go to the background argument to establish precise definitions of the words we are using—we might all get into an interminable debate: "What do you mean by *wrong?*" "Someone not qualified for the job!" "How are you defining 'qualified'?" etc. I will try to show the precise nature of the background argument behind the shorthand and, in doing so, I will show the precise definitions of "right" and "wrong," "good" and "bad."

This shorthand can also be misused against a benchmark of co-herence in a way that causes confusion and unintended anger. And when it is, there can be a lot of trouble between the speaker and the listener; trouble that can quickly get out of hand. For not only does the misused shorthand cause confusion, but the listener—unaware of the nature of the shorthand and its background argu-ment—is unable to name the error being made, and, confused and frustrated, may end up throwing angry words at the speaker.

By the end of chapter one I shall have constructed a model of the shorthand and the background argument against which we shall be able to examine many statements that occur in nonmoral de-cision-making situations. I shall try to show, by specific examples, how well the shorthand works when it is being used correctly, and all the trouble it can cause when it is used incorrectly.

In chapter two, with this model and the precise definitions of "right" and "wrong," "good" and "bad" in hand, I shall begin to explore morality. I intend to show that while moral discourse is substantively different from nonmoral discourse in one respect, *it is identical in all other respects*, Here, too, we find a shorthand ("Murder is wrong," "Stealing is wrong") that is related to a complex background argument: here, too, we find the same precise definitions of the words "right" and "wrong," "good" and "bad" when the shorthand is being used correctly; and indeed, up and down the structure of the model—with one difference—everything we found in chapter one will be found in moral discourse as well.

In chapter three, with this model and these definitions still in hand, I shall explore the misuse of the shorthand as it occurs in moral discourse and show that this misuse not only causes anger but is, I believe, partly responsible for some of the worst excesses that man has perpetrated on man in the name of *right*. By the end of this chapter I think we shall have a pretty good idea of what morality is, what it is not, and why our misunderstanding of it generates so much passion.

Chapter One

The Hybrid

The Logical Positivists and their counterparts in ethics—the emotivists—met with a peculiar fate. Central to their argument was the verification principle,* which they applied to various kinds of statements found in the objective grammatical form

---

*"The Logical Positivists were not, as philosophers, concerned with the truth or falsehood of scientific statements; this they held, rightly, to be the affair of the scientists. Their proper concern, as philosophers, was held to be with *meaning*. Accordingly, the criterion they devised was to be a test of meaningfulness or significance, a test which the sciences would pass and metaphysics would not. This criterion became known as the Verification Principle. . . . We can say roughly that what the principle laid down was this: that the meaning of any statement is shown by the way in which it could be verified—it being assumed that verification must always at least terminate in empirical observation, or sense-experience. A special exception was made in favor of such analytic formulae as those of mathematics, which do not require to be empirically verified." G. J. Warnock, *English Philosophy Since 1900* (New York: Oxford University Press, 1966), p. 30.

According to the emotivists, "When we say 'This pie is good' or 'This act is right,' we seem to be making an assertion just as we are when we say 'This pie is round' or 'That act is deliberate.' But actually such expressions, which appear to be asserting ethical predicates, do not, like the others, serve to give information at all but rather to *vent an emotion* or to evoke an attitude." Philip Blair Rice, *On the Knowledge of Good and Evil* (New York: Random House, 1955), p. 60 (emphasis added).

(e.g., "Arsenic is a poison," "God is good," "Stealing is wrong"), and then they dismissed as nonsense all statements they could not verify (e.g., "God is good," "Stealing is wrong"). In doing so, they came under fierce attack from moralists, theologians, and other philosophers, yet they remained surprisingly unscathed. By the post-World War II years, however, they were all but ignored and forgotten, as if the attacks on them had been successful, after all, and there was nothing more to say. Indeed, I don't think it would be stretching matters to say that today the Logical Positivists stand discredited even though no one has actually discredited them.

The Positivists, I believe, did make a dreadful error and deserved to be discredited, but their critics dismissed them without pointing out their actual error, and a lot was lost to philosophy as a result. The error was *not* the verification principle itself—this is just what philosophy, so often drifting toward vague talk, needed and still needs. The error was in the application of the principle by the Positivists themselves.

Wittgenstein said in the preface to *Tractatus*, "The whole sense of the book might be summed up in the following words: what can be said at all can be said clearly and what we cannot talk about we must consign to silence."* And then, in the body of the book: "The correct method in philosophy would really be the following: to say nothing except what can be said, i.e., the propositions of natural science. . . ."† With these two statements Wittgenstein committed and summed up the basic error of the Positivists, who were so bewitched by the remarkable achievements of science that they failed to do what they set out to do. Rather than painstakingly analyze the meaning of various kinds of statements found in the objective grammatical form to see which kind are, in fact, verifiable, the Positivists tossed *all nonscientific statements* into the nonsense bin, and, in so doing tossed an important subclass of nonscientific statements—in this book I will call them *hybrid statements*—into the wrong bin. Hybrid statements are related to

---

*Ludwig Wittgenstein, *Tractatus*, translated by O. F. Pears and B. F. McGuinness, (London: Routledge and Kegan Paul, 1961), p. 3.

†Ibid., p. 151.

our desires, and for this reason, among others, they are unlike any statements found in science; but like scientific statements they are in the objective grammatical form, which is where they belong, since they are also true and verifiable. (It is because of this mixed ancestry that I call them hybrids.)

The error the Positivists made is understandable. Many statements related to desire, but put in the objective grammatical form, are properly exposed as meaningless and nonsensical in terms of anything objective or true/false verifiable. Time and again when we say "It is right . . ." or "It is good . . ." we mean nothing more than "I want . . ." or "I like . . . " However, there is this exception: the hybrid—a statement related to desire that not only looks objective and verifiable, but is, even though it is far different from statements found in science, or even in the struggling sciences—history, sociology, psychology, and anthropology.

In my introduction I said that we often use a shorthand in nonmoral discourse when the speaker and the listener share the same desire (e.g., that their company make a profit), and when a decision has to be made relevant to this desire (e.g., there is a vacancy in the accounting department that has to be filled). *The hybrid statement is a form of this shorthand,* and indeed, the hybrid is found only in the situation where we have a shared desire and a decision to be made relevant to it. I also said that this shorthand is often used incorrectly against a benchmark of coherence. When this happens we get what I will call the *false hybrid,* a statement that looks identical in grammatical form to the hybrid statement but is entirely different in meaning. (How can we possibly tell the difference?—by going to the background argument, as we shall see.) In this chapter I shall explore the hybrid and the false hybrid when they are employed in nonmoral discourse. Later I shall explore them as they are found in moral discourse. I might just add at this point that I do not believe that the hybrid statement could have been isolated without the modern theory of computers and the discovery of what has come to be known as probabilistic logic. I believe that for centuries philosophers simply could not have discovered the hybrid because they did not have the tools necessary for its discovery—all of which should become clearer as we go along.*

A BASIC TRUTH

While hybrid statements are extremely common, they are but a small expression of a basic truth—namely, that we have desires and know how to satisfy some of them. This truth is so obvious that until very recently it has hardly been mentioned by philosophers, much less explored. Indeed, it has been only in the past few years that philosophers have turned their concentrated attention to the concepts of desire and fulfillment, and have begun—tentatively—to bring in the rich harvest of truth that has always been there for the taking.†

Theologians were embarrassed by their desires and philosophers generally ignored them, except to disparage them as impositions upon reason and truth. I have often wondered if it wasn't the father of modern philosophy, the elegant and cautious Descartes, who got us heading in the wrong direction to begin with. Ever mindful of the Church, Descartes—in searching for what he knew most certain in the universe—gave us, in "Cogito, ergo sum," something really quite muzzy as a basic truth, when, had

---

*In *Tractatus* (op. cit., p. 37) Wittgenstein said, "The tacit conventions on which the understanding of everyday language depends are enormously complicated." That is a precise summary of the argument I shall be making, but Wittgenstein, having come up with this insight, could not have grasped the crucial concept of what he meant by "tacit conventions." These conventions are, I believe, made possible by the mind's computerlike ability to encode and decode what are actually extremely long arguments into a few spoken words—and Wittgenstein was simply unaware of what we now know about computers and the mind's computerlike abilities.

†See Michael Bratman, "Intention and Means-End Reasoning," *Philosophical Review* 92 (1981): 252-65; Joseph Raz, "Reasons for Action, Decisions, and Norms," *Mind* 84 (1975): 481-99; and Bruce Aune, *Reason and Action* (Dordrecht, Holland: Reidel, 1977). In moral philosophy, interest in desire has had a slightly longer history, and Ralph Barton Perry (*General Theory of Value,* Cambridge: Harvard University Press, 1926) came tantalizingly close to uncovering desire's true relationship to morality and to making my argument.

he been more frank and worked harder on the problem—say, six or seven straight hours—he might have shouted in Latin, "What I know most certain is that I am hungry!" and then, but no longer shouting, "What I know second most certain is how to satisfy my hunger." But desire* has been too earthy for lofty seekers after truth, even if desire is what we know most certain; and even if our ability to satisfy some of our desires is our most certain link between mind and world.

The hybrid statement, although used countless times each day in ordinary discourse, is but a minor manifestation of the basic truth that we have desires and know how to satisfy some of them; the major manifestation is that a hundred times a day each of us, silently and alone, satisfies strings of desires with knowledge gained from past experience—e.g., to illuminate a room, to find the faucet, to quench our thirst, to plunge the room into total darkness again—and each of us does it with as much confidence, certainty, and success as any scientist knows or has proved about anything.† Indeed, what scientist—if pushed to the wall—would not acknowledge that he or she was more certain of his or her hunger and thirst and how to satisfy them than of the second law of thermodynamics or even that $1 - 1 = 0$?

GENERAL FEATURES OF THE HYBRID

While these desires that we silently and successfully satisfy are, I

---

*While the word "hunger" is often used synonymously for desire it is not, technically, a desire but an unpleasant sensation that causes us to want food. But there is no need to be too technical here; my point is that hunger or the desire to eat is as real a thing as we will ever know.

†Although I have hardly begun to explain the nature of the hybrid statement, I have said that is is unique in that it is nonscientific *and* verifiable. What, then, is the nature of the silent truths I have just been discussing? I would say that it is scientific and that if, in quenching our thirst, we actually talked to ourselves we would find the statements we made were factual and similar to the statements found in science—this switch will illuminate the room, that faucet supplies water, etc., with the final statement being the sense data observation, "My thirst is quenched."

believe, extremely important to philosophy—leading, perhaps, to an epistemology that will shame all others in its scope and certainty—my concern in this book will be with a different class of desires: those that require us to say something for their satisfaction or that are more easily satisfied by saying something.

In this realm of desire, which may encompass half or more of all words spoken, there are three basic subdivisions: "I want" statements, "Some of us what" statements; and "We [all] want" statements. There is the possibility of truth in all these statements —a way of getting what we want by saying something. *But if it is not our intention to deceive, confuse, or infuriate,* then only in the third case can we legitimately set aside "we" and "want' and use the objective grammatical form; in the other cases the only legitimate way to say what is on our minds is to say it—"I want . . ." "Some of us want. . . ."* Let me, for now, concentrate on the third case, for it here that we find the hybrid.

The hybrid statement is, above all else, related to desire—*a shared desire.* Let me quickly define this term as I shall use it: a shared desire is one that (1) requires us to work with other people for its satisfaction (e.g., to build a skyscraper) and that the speaker and the listener hold, or (2) is held by the speaker and the listener (e.g., not to be fired, to be respected by one's peers) but may or may not require them to work together to satisfy. It is in the nature of a shared desire, as I shall use the

---

*It is not my intention to lecture "vigorous game players" who rely on deceiving and confusing others in order to achieve their ends, for that would be a task beyond the goals of this book. My argument will only be that if it is not one's intention to deceive or confuse then one must be aware of both the correct and the incorrect use of the hybrid form, for to put what is essentially an "I want . . ." or a "Some of us want . . ." argument in the objective grammatical form (i.e., in the hybrid form) can be terribly deceptive and confusing; it can and does lead to all sorts of problems. This is what I mean when I use the words "legitimate" and "illegitimate" to describe sentences that do or do not reflect the true argument. Looked at another way, my concern is not with changing the ways of "vigorous game players" or even charlatans, but with the innocent— those who do not wish to confuse or deceive. I cannot deny, however, that on my agenda is the goal of making the innocent less gullible to the words of charlatans.

term, that everyone in the group of speakers and listeners can assume, based on the very nature of the group, that most everyone else in the group has it. There is always the possibility, particularly in large groups, of "atypics"—those who, while physically in the group, don't share the desires of the group—but I shall get to them later. A shared desire is, obviously, a common desire (within a group), but all common desires are not necessarily shared. Everyone may desire to be team captain, but they can't work together to satisfy it, and in fact this desire puts them all at odds.

The hybrid statement is elliptic in the extreme, and it sits atop a complex background argument that has, at best, been only vaguely understood for what it is. When I use the word "hybrid" I mean both the spoken statement and its background argument. The "spoken hybrid" or the "hybrid statement" is the spoken part of the hybrid, and the "background argument" or the "extended argument" is the unspoken part. Except for its objective grammatical form, the hybrid statement doesn't look at all like the statements of science; nevertheless, it is verifiable, just as if it were a scientific statement. To verify the hybrid statement we must go to the background argument, which, as I have said, is only vaguely understood—and this raises the question of how, in ordinary discourse, we verify the speaker's statement. The answer, to be more fully explained later on, is that we *don't actually verify* it; instead, we have an all-but-palpable *feel* for its truth.

The background argument is a successful meld of facts, desires, and verifiable propositions into a logically compelling conclusion: *this* is the best way to satisfy the shared desire. The spoken hybrid is the bottom line; it gives us the right decision without all the background argument. Sometimes, however, an element of the background argument is added to the spoken hybrid to help in verification.

Roughly speaking, here is how it works in practice: a question is raised, a decision has to be made, someone figures out the right answer and issues the hybrid statement; the listener(s) may or may not ask for some supporting evidence; the speaker presents one or two elements from the background argument; everyone is in agreement on the truth being spoken (people *sense* the truth of the background argument); the right decision is made (the one that holds the *best chance* of satisfying the shared desire); and people go about their business—which for some or all may be to carry out the decision or the right decision may be to do nothing. It is in the nature of hybrids that, generally speaking, their use does not cause problems, speaker to listener; they are dull, boring, uninteresting truths that like our currency are used successfully many times each day without being examined. In part it is their uninterestingness and the ease of their usage that has caused them to be ignored.

There is also, however, the false hybrid—a statement that looks just like a hybrid, but doesn't have a hybrid argument behind it. This statement looks as if it is true/false verifiable (it, too, is in the objective grammatical form) but is outside the realm of verification. Such statements are very interesting in that their use raises all sorts of problems and they are forever being analyzed, but they cannot be understood and the problems they cause cannot be eased until we first understand their "uninteresting" opposites, the hybrids.

Between the hybrid and the false hybrid there is a narrow area that might be called the *questionable hybrid*. But generally speaking, once we go to the background argument we will know whether we have the makings of a hybrid or not, and if we don't, *there is no question*—we don't have a hybrid. Examples of hybrids and false hybrids that I will examine in this and subsequent chapters are:

- Jones is the wrong man for the job.
- It's a beautiful day.
- Tommy is a bad child.
- Murder is wrong.
- Abortion is wrong.

And, to repeat: we won't know whether we have a hybrid or a false hybrid until we go to the background argument behind each of them.

THE JONES HYBRID

Let us start, then, with a hybrid, and an example in which the background argument, while complex, is about as simple as we are likely to find. Take the statement "Jones is the wrong man for the job; we ought not to hire him." Let us assume that you are my boss and you have asked me to screen candidates for an accounting job, and that Jones is one of them. (I will bring in other candidates later on, all of whom happen to be men, to make things easier for me grammatically.) Hovering in the background of our discussion and your ultimate decision are many desires,* but let me select three that are *generally shared*† in (although not all of them exclusive to) the world of business, and let us assume that you and I share them too: (1) we want to keep our jobs; (2) we want to be respected by our peers: and (3) we want our company to prosper. I might just add at this point that a hybrid truth is always relative to a particular "world" of shared desires. Therefore, it will help readers to appreciate the argument that follows if they cheerfully accept the role and desires that I have assigned, regardless of their true sentiments toward employment, business, or capitalism. In other words, pretend, if you will, to be

---

*Such is the newness of the philosopher's interest in desire as something important to our understanding of things that I find myself in the odd position of having to provide footnotes in support of the obvious (for fear of being accused of having stolen someone else's idea). Thus I want to say, in passing, that having a desire and intending to fulfill it are, of course, two diffeent matters ("I would love to play pro ball, but I am going to medical school instead"). This is, however, a major point in Michael Bratman's article, which I have cited. He writes, "Intentions are psychological events that are distinct from desires" (p. 256). But proving or disproving the obvious is in the very nature of philosophy, and let me say that I took considerable encouragement from Bratman's paper and from the fact that desire was being taken seriously in a philosophical journal. And one final point: It seems to me that when we use the word "desire," the context often indicates our intention to fulfill it, and when this is the case I won't bother with the distinction between desire and the intention to fulfill it.

† In the discussion that immediately follows I will use several phrases whose meanings are pretty apparent but which I shall explain and define more fully further on. Until then I'll put these phrases in italics.

a hard-headed business person. Later on, I'll excuse the reader from this role and address some of the nonbusiness concerns that may arise as I unfold this first example of the hybrid.

Let us also assume that the three shared desires are of such importance to us that we are unwilling to take any *obvious risk* of frustrating them; that we are reasonably informed business people, which is to say that through education and experience we have gained a fair idea of how things work in the world of business; that there are plenty of candidates for the accounting job from which to choose; and, finally, that neither one of us has a *singular and secret desire* that will be satisfied or frustrated by the decision concerning Jones. (He has not promised me $10,000 if he gets the job.)

A third party calls me with some information about Jones, and after verifying it, I rush into your office and say, "Jones is the wrong man for the accounting job! We ought not to hire him." You ask me why, and I say because he has twice been convicted of embezzlement. You explode with laughter and say, "Jones *is* the wrong man for the job; a *truer statement was never made!*" Case closed. But why? How did we so quickly jump from an "is" (twice-convicted embezzler) to an "ought"? Is our conclusion, at heart, objective or subjective? Is it an imperative in the objective grammatical form? Is it an emotive—a statement in the objective form that is really no more than an expression of emotion—for example, "I don't like Jones"? Is it cognitive or noncognitive? Is it a judgment or an opinion? Is it verifiable, and if so, how? Unless we bring in our shared desires, questions like these can ensnare us hopelessly; but once we do invoke shared desires, they can all be answered.

My *statement on Jones is a hybrid,** and it is elliptic in the extreme, but laying out the background elements, we get this compelling argument:

Given what we know about how things work in the world of business, we run an *obvious risk* of frustrating desires that are important to us if we knowingly hire a two-time embezzler for an accounting job, and since we wish to take *no risk* of frustrating

---

*The actual spoken hybrid is "Jones is the wrong man for the job." The phrase ". . . we ought not to hire him" is something else that I'll get to when I discuss the meaning of "ought" statements.

these desires, it would be wrong, incorrect, and incoherent *of us* to hire Jones.*

Or, looking at the argument schematically:

Fact:	Jones is a two-time embezzler.
Shared Desires:	To keep our jobs, to be respected, to have our company prosper.
Verifiable Proposition:	Those who knowingly hire a two-time embezzler run an *obvious risk* of being fired, being held up to ridicule, and ruining their company.
Conclusion:	Given our various desires, and our intention to take no *obvious risk* of frustrating them—it would be wrong, incorrect, and incoherent *of us* to hire Jones.

While the logic here is compelling, it is clearly not the logic of "Socrates is a man; all men are mortal; therefore, Socrates is mortal." But still it is logic—probabilistic logic. We are never certain what will happen in a given case, but very nearly certain what will happen, *on average*, in a large number of cases, and this average we get from past experience or experiments. Thus, what is true is not that we will be fired if we hire Jones, but that one particular decision holds the *best possibility* of our not being fired.

Some observations on the Jones hybrid and hybrids in general:

- With the hybrid we are in a wonderful world where almost everyone shares the same desire; where past experience clearly in-

---

*Whether or not embezzlement is immoral remains to be seen, but in any case, morality was not part of our considerations, because I don't believe that most business people would raise a question of morality in this situation. This is not to preclude the possibility of someone's raising the question of the moral implications of hiring or not hiring a two-time embezzler, even though he has paid his debts to society. Indeed, I will raise both of these questions further on.

dicates the best chance of satisfying the desire or avoiding having it frustrated; and where what we say and what we hear are all in harmony with our inner beliefs. The reason is that we all *sense* the same compelling background argument that stands behind the spoken words, even though we are unaware of many of the elements and logical connections inherent in the argument. I use the word "sense" because what we get with the hybrid statement is an all-but-physical feel for its truth—the feeling that *this* decision is the *best possible* decision that we can make! (The Jones hybrid was negative, but hybrids can be positive as well. In most of the arguments that follow, however, I will call on negative examples, since they are easier to deal with. Generally speaking, it is easier to recognize a decision that will lead to disaster than one that will guarantee success. For example, there may not be a right man or woman for the accounting job in the hybrid sense.)

• Buried deep in every hybrid argument is value—something important to us, something we want or want to keep (our jobs, our reputations, the success of our company). Furthermore, the shared desire or value may well be subject to judgment from other people or groups who may not share our values and may not want us to have what we want. And, along this same line, the shared nature of a desire or value doesn't make it moral, as we shall see. The point is that the hybrid statement has a strictly mechanical job to do, and as such it accepts the shared desire *as a given*. (Even the devil and his assistants can form hybrids!) Which is to say that within the context of a hybrid argument the desire is absolute, which is further to say that fulfilling it, or taking no *obvious risk* of frustrating it, is assumed*—speaker to listener —and is paramount. If the desire is not shared or if other con-

---

*Since I have already said that speakers and listeners are only vaguely aware of the argument behind the spoken hybrid, we must also conclude that in rapid-fire, shorthand talk we may not even be aware that at the heart of what we are saying is desire. Indeed, if a longer explanation is called for by a listener, desire may not even be brought up; but instead, the speaker just builds words on words, and there is static, confusion, and anger as a key element (desire) is not recognized and therefore not stated.

cerns, considerations, or desires creep into our discussion, then we must first address and settle them before we put *anything* in the objective form—assuming our intention is not to deceive, confuse, or infuriate. In short, we cannot use the objective hybrid form (which implies a hybrid argument behind it) if we don't have all the elements necessary to form a hybrid.

• The reader may have observed that while "wrong" is an adjective modifying "man" in the spoken hybrid, in the extended argument the terms "wrong," "incorrect," and "incoherent" would apply to *us or our decision* if we hire Jones. This fast and loose play with words is typical of the spoken hybrid, and needless to say, it can create endless problems if, in trying to get at the meaning of specific words, we examine only the words being spoken.

We could spend a lifetime trying to define the word "wrong" in "wrong man" and never reach agreement. Only by going to the background argument do we realize that what Jones is, is a matter of *fact* (he is a two-time embezzler), and it is *we* who are wrong, incorrect, and incoherent if we think we can hire him and not risk frustrating desires that are of major importance to us. In other words, "wrong" has a precise definition when used in a hybrid—it means incorrect and incoherent of us to do, given our intention to satisfy a shared desire or criterion. Jones *is* the wrong man for the job, in a manner of speaking, but it is a manner of speaking, and must be understood as such if we are to get at the true meaning of the Jones statement.

• In the discussion ahead I will be concentrating on the words "right" and "wrong," but let me examine quickly, at this point, the words "good" and "bad" and their precise definitions. Here, too, the words tend to jump their nouns when we go to the background argument. In the spoken statement, for example, "good" or "bad" often modify a person, but in the background argument they modify the risk or chance that something will happen if we make a particular decision. Thus I might have said, "Jones is a bad candidate" and, the background argument would be, "Given our shared desires . . . there is an unacceptable, or bad, risk that they will be frustrated if we hire Jones." In short, in a hybrid statement, "good" means "a favorable chance" and "bad" means "an unacceptable risk."

As if this were not complex enough, the words "right," "wrong," "good," and "bad" *have another set of precise definitions* outside of, or prior to, decision-making situations. *These words can describe acts that are, or are not, in keeping with a group's generally shared desires.* Countless times each day bad or wrong acts are committed, given a group's generally shared desires—from sneaking ahead of other people in line to falling asleep during an important business meeting, from double-parking to drunk driving—and while some of these acts (for reasons that I will explain further on) may demand a decision, a bad act or doing something wrong does not automatically demand that a decision be made, for there are simply too many of these acts to handle. So, too, with good acts or doing something right—the fact that it was your presentation that won the new account does not automatically require that you be given a raise or a promotion. But for now let me return to the hybrid—to situations where we must make a decision; where "right" means correct and coherent, and "wrong" means incorrect and incoherent of us to do given our intention of satisfying a generally shared desire; and where "good" means a favorable chance and "bad" means an unfavorable risk of our desires being satisfied or frustrated.

CONFIRMATION, VERIFICATION, AND QUANTIFICATION

Hybrid statements are true statements. They are also verifiable. When we go to the background argument, we are logically compelled to the conclusion that *this decision* holds the best possibility of satisfying our shared desire, and that is the truth. However, before a hybrid statement is offered or accepted, both the speaker and the listener must confirm, verify, and quantify the various elements in the background argument. And, although you were not aware of it, your mind—in possession as it is of a marvelous "computer" (or, technically, in possession of computerlike capabilities)—did just this in the *fraction of a second* between my uttering the word "embezzlement" and your explosive laugh.

While you were unaware of all the computations being made (it all happened so fast) and were probably unaware of how the "computer" was figuring—I don't know either, but I will attempt to *deduce* how it must have been working—nevertheless, you were given (by the "computer") a powerful feel (an electric jolt, if you will) for the truth of the Jones statement. Unfortunately, this "computer" is capable of short-circuiting and giving us the same feel or jolt for statements that are *not verifiable*—the same feel or jolt for the false hybrid—as we shall see. Let us now examine, by deduction, how the "computer" must be working when it is working well.

• The alleged fact in the Jones hybrid can or cannot be confirmed (if he has been convicted twice of embezzlement, then a record exists somewhere for our examination). Obviously, in the split second when your "computer" made its calculations, it did not confirm the fact, but it did confirm the probability of its truth sufficiently for your purposes. It considered my status as underling to you, and hireling in the corporate structure; it noted that I was in dead earnest; it recalled my past trustworthiness and reliability; and, most important, it projected that I would be in deep trouble not only if I were lying about Jones (and it came out, as well it might) but if I were simply passing on hearsay.

In short, while the basic fact was not confirmed, I was confirmed as a legitimate secondary source of confirmation—and this was relayed to you as a feeling of trust in me and in my words.

• While every element in the background argument is essential to the formation of a hybrid, the shared or *generally shared* desire is first among equals. It is ultimately the *sharedness* of the desire or criterion or thing important to us or value (our jobs, etc.) that makes the hybrid objective. It is the sharedness of a value that can make a value objective. In the world of business most employees don't want to be fired, or be a laughingstock, or have their company fold; their jobs, reputations, and company are of value or importance to them—and that's the truth.

The "computer" takes a lot of information about the group

we are in (based on our past experiences) and quantifies the number of people in the group who share the desire or desires relevant to the decision before us, and if the figure is anything but *extremely high** the "computer" gives us a feel that we don't have the makings of a hybrid and if we don't wish to deceive, confuse, or infuriate, we slip comfortably into an alternative nonhybrid way of talking that I will explain further on.

I don't know what the actual figure is for business people not wanting to be fired (or to be a laughingstock or to see their company ruined), but I have made the assumption, and I think it is a fair assumption, that the figure is *extremely high* (say 99.9 percent). Therefore business people can communicate rapidly (and form hybrids) on the basis of this shared desire without running into problems. (In every group, particularly in every large group, there is, as I have said before, the possibility of "atypics"—those who don't share the generally shared desires of the group—and I will get to them below.)

• Hybrid statements are true and verifiable: when we go to the complex background argument we are logically compelled to the truth that, given past experience, this decision holds the best possible chance of satisfying or not frustrating our shared desires. But the complex background argument is very different from arguments and proofs found in science in that it contains desires and values. However, among the many elements in the background argument of a hybrid *there is always a verifiable proposition* that is akin to the propositions of science, and to their method of verification (for example, those who knowingly hire a two-time embezzler for an accounting job run an *obvious risk* of being

---

*In probabilistic logic it is often necessary to coin less-than-precise terms (e.g., "extremely high" and "obvious risk"); it is in the very nature of the work if we want to get any work done and not be bogged down endlessly defining and qualifying. Quantum mechanics, meteorology, and even advanced mathematics are replete with such terms—"disorderly systems," "low entropy," "quasithermo-dynamical considerations," "the theory of large numbers," "a good chance of rain later in the week." That these words and phrases cannot be precisely defined is not argument-threatening—we can still get a lot of work done with them. Nevertheless, I will refine "extremely high" and "obvious risk" in a moment.

fired).* The kinship is closer to quantum mechanics and meteorology than to the clockwork precision of Newtonian physics. But in all cases—quantum mechanics, Newtonian physics, and the hybrid —what is true is not that something will happen in the future, but the frequency with which it happened in the past, and we assume that it will happen with the same frequency in the future.

Or, if there is no evidence from the past to examine, we may be able to set up experiments that, once conducted, become evidence from the past, and we go on the assumption that under similar conditions this frequency (including 100 percent in the case of Newtonian physics) will hold in the future.

In short, while hybrid arguments are verifiable, they are different from scientific arguments in that they contain such elements as value—things important to us; however, the background argument itself always contains a verifiable proposition that is similar to the propositions of science.

With the hybrid, however, sometimes there is a problem in verifying the proposition, unlike verification in science: The proposition may be so widely held to be true that it creates a reality where there is no evidence to support it. And, as a practical matter, experiments are not possible. For example, the proposition that convicted embezzlers are obviously greater risks to embezzle in the future than are individuals who have never embezzled (a proposition that your "computer" employed) is so widely held to be true that few embezzlers are knowingly hired for accounting jobs, and the number of two-time embezzlers who are knowingly hired is probably close to nil. All of which means that—strictly speaking—we have no evidence that we will be fired or be held up to ridicule if we hire Jones, and as a practical matter, experiments are out of the question.

Nevertheless, we are not without resources. We could, for example, conduct a poll among bosses and ask them what they would think of, and what they would do with, an employee who

---

*Given *any* desire, even the secret and singular desire to burn down the company headquarters, there are these same kinds of verifiable propositions that we can call on that will aid us in our task (e.g., gasoline ignites more quickly than home heating oil). But if the desire is not shared then we don't have the makings of a hybrid.

knowingly hired a two-time embezzler for an accounting job. My bet would be that such a poll would give us a high figure for being fired and being held up to ridicule, and that such a figure would not only suggest an *obvious risk* to everyone but would also indicate that an extremely high percentage of business people would find the risk unacceptable and totally out of the question.

As for the proposition that two-time embezzlers are much greater risks to embezzle again (on which all the other arguments actually rest), it would probably not be difficult to determine the risk involved in hiring convicted embezzlers, leaving aside two-time embezzlers as such. If 5 percent of all embezzlers have embezzled before and if .005 percent of the adult population has been convicted of embezzlement, then embezzlers, as a class, are a thousand times more likely to embezzle in the future than adults in general. If it turned out that embezzlers are no significant risk to embezzle again, then this would be fascinating information, since it contradicts a widely held assumption (and our "computer" would have to undergo a major reprogramming). But until this finding was widely disseminated and accepted, we—as business people—would have to be cautious of how we used it.

As for Jones, we do not know, of course, that he will embezzle again, but short of remarkable and extenuating circumstances surrounding his two convictions, we had better assume he is typical of his class, and short of widely disseminated and accepted evidence to the contrary, we had better assume his class is a far greater risk to embezzle than those who have never embezzled— given our various desires. All this the "computer" did.

If there are any lingering philosophical doubts about the truth of the Jones hybrid, they can be quickly dispelled by hiring him and observing what happens. In all probability we shall be fired on the spot, and be the laughingstock of the businss community. (Specifically, upon hearing what we have done, other business people will burst out laughing—venting their relief that we don't work for them.) Or, to put the matter in a way pleasing to the Logical Positivists—i.e., using strictly sense data—if we utter the words "You're hired" to Jones, there is a high probability we will subsequently hear the words "You're fired," and laughter.

• When we lay out the background argument in a negative hybrid, we find an "obvious risk," one that is above and beyond the normal risks of living, working, and making decisions. It is not unlike a meteorologist's small-craft warning—the meteorologist is not saying that you will sink if you go out in a rowboat, but that based on past experience and current weather conditions the probability is greater than normal that you will. It is true that all meteorologists don't issue their warnings under the same weather conditions, *but it is also true that there is a weather condition under which all have issued them.* In a similar manner, everyone may not see a risk (in which case it is not obvious) at the same point, but it is true that there is a point at which almost everyone (with the same desire) will, indicating there are, in fact, obvious risks.

The "computer" quantifies the risk, but it need not be high to be obvious. The risk of getting killed playing Russian roulette is only 16.66 percent (with a six-shooter), yet it is obvious to everyone, including those playing the game, since there isn't much point to the game beyond the risk.

However, the *unacceptability of the risk* (e.g., the risk of getting fired if we hire a two-time embezzler) must be extremely high for the group we are working in, and the "computer" calculates this as well. If only 80 percent are unwilling to take the risk, this means that one in five potential listeners is willing to take the risk, and this is bound to cause trouble if we talk in the objective hybrid form, *for essential to the hybrid argument is the general acceptance of all its elements.*

Despite these many caveats, qualifications, and potential problems, the hybrid is a marvel of probabilistic logic that successfully gets *Homo sapiens* through countless decisions each day. When the "computer" works well, it works extremely well and gives us a jolt of truth for the right decision, the one that holds the *best chance* of satisfying the shared desire—even though we don't understand what is going on.

JUDGING WORLDS

We won't be in a position to judge worlds—the world of business, the world of medicine, the underworld, the world of sports, the world of politics—and the shared desires and values that prevail in them until we explore the concepts of opinion and morality. Nevertheless, let me say at this point that it has not been my intention to prejudice the reader or anyone else from saying "Capitalism is a mean and rotten institution that brings out the worst in everyone" or "It is not fair to reject Jones; he has paid his debts to society." The speaker may even be in business for himself; if he is, he doesn't need to say anything to anyone, he can just hire Jones, and I, for one—unemployed and of liberal inclination —will applaud. My only intention has been to take a somewhat realistic example from a real world of generally shared desires, and to try to show the existence, within this world, of statements that don't look like the factual statement found in science (except for their objective form) but are, in fact, verifiable. To repeat: The hybrid has a job to do but the job is not to judge the values on which it is founded.

THE HYBRID AND THE GROUP

While the word "world" covers what I want to cover much of the time, namely, a formal or informal association of individuals who have at least one shared desire that they can work together toward satisfying—I will for the most part refer to "groups" in the arguments to come. For I want to include two individuals who have come together in even an ephemeral association—say, to climb a mountain, or to rob a bank, and who must make decisions based on their shared desire to get safely up and down or to have a lot of instant cash—and the word "world" is a trifle much for such passing associations.

Without hybrids, groups would be impossible. Specifically, without the elliptic hybrid statement, vital decision-making would be fatally protracted—leading to the frustration of the shared desire, and to the demise of the group. Which is to say that we must make the kind of assumptions we do make in forming hybrids. If we could not assume that listeners shared the desire central to our hybrid, we would first have to ask them, which would take long enough in itself. But then, having found that out, if we had to begin every remark with "Given our shared desire . . . to keep our company solvent . . . to reach the top of the mountain . . . to win the championship . . . to rob a bank . . ." nothing would ever get done on time. In other words, in decision-making situations we drop pronouns and verbs; don't mention our guiding criterion or desire;* put adjectives together with nouns they don't modify in the background argument; make calculations based on verifiable propositions that we don't actually verify; and omit long sequences of argumentation, all to hurry things along. It doesn't matter much of the time that, with all this omitting, we have lost sight of what we are actually talking about; the "computer" takes care of everything and gives us a jolt of truth in favor of the correct decision.

In the realm of desires, decisions, and fulfillment the elliptic hybrid statement is not simply a convenient way of expressing our thoughts; it is essential if we are to work together and satisfy desires that are important to us and that we can't satisfy on our own. Needless to say, all this assuming—as necessary as it is—can lead to trouble on occasion.

I have alluded to the possibility of this trouble by using the phrase "generally shared desire." In any group—particularly in any large group—there is always the possibility of saboteurs, psychotics, spies, thieves, and other atypics† who, while physically in the group, do not share the generally shared desires of the group and may, in fact, be out to frustrate them (e.g., the employee who wants to ruin the company because he or she has taken a short

---

*While criterion and desire are not synonymous, they are, I believe, pretty much interchangeable in decision-making situations. A criterion, by definition, is a guide to action, but a desire that we intend to satisfy is also a guide to action. Looked at from the other direction, if we have established a criterion and intend to follow it, then we also have a desire—namely, to follow the criterion when it is applicable in decision-making situations. Why we have criteria (and, I might add, principles and maxims) is an interesting question and probably related to the group's—or, for example, a parent's—desire to control and guide behavior when the group or parent is not available for guidance and supervision (e.g., a parent saying to a child, "Never cross against a red light)."

†A shared desire isn't morally good just because it is shared, which means, among other things, that being an atypic doesn't make one immoral.

position in the company's shares). Despite these possibilities, we *can and must* dismiss them in ordinary discourse, because the number of atypics in any group is always small. If the number were large, we would have a badly divided group in the process of breaking up, where nothing could be assumed anyway. That we sometimes get in trouble is something we can guard against to some degree, but too much guarding against trouble will slow everything down and lead to its own problems.

A corollary to this point is that the truth of a hybrid doesn't evaporate just because a particular listener doesn't share the generally shared desire on which the hybrid is founded. Jones is still the wrong man for the job even if the particular employee I am talking to secretly wants to ruin the company because he or she has taken a short position in the company's shares. If this saboteur has a partner, it is also true that between them—and in private—they can form any number of hybrids from their shared desire to ruin the company, including "Jones is the right man for the job, in fact he's perfect!" (These conspirators are in a world of their own.)

However, if half the employees in our company want to ruin it, or be fired, or be a laughingstock, then hybrid truths will be impossible; indeed, in such a weird situation ordinary communication will be impossible, and the company will quickly fall apart.

CAN "IS" LEAD TO "OUGHT"?

I said in the introduction that (with one important exception) moral discourse and nonmoral discourse are similar as far as they occur in decision-making situations involving two or more individuals—for both rely upon a shorthand; the basic words "right" and "wrong," "good" and "bad" have the same precise definitions; the logic of the arguments is the same; and there is also the same kind of misuse of the shorthand and the basic words. I am a long way from proving this. But I can now show that (with the one exception) this up-and-down-the-line similarity does hold for "ought" statements as they are found in both moral and nonmoral decision-making situations. I bring up the matter now in order to finish my formal analysis of the Jones hybrid, where the reader may have observed that while the word "ought" was found in the spoken statement, it disappeared in the background argument—and the reader may have wondered what happened to it. I also asked how we so quickly got from an "is" (twice-convicted embezzler) to an "ought" ("we ought not to hire him") but did not actually explain how we did.

The reason we did not find the word "ought" in the background argument is that in or out of morality, I have found it far too treacherous a word to be used in attempts at precise analysis. Indeed, I do not believe the word itself can be defined (as it is used in decision-making situations), although we can come to understand the meaning of an "ought" statement. And while I am on the subject of "ought," I want to present a major argument in modern moral philosophy (an argument relevant to my argument) that has been given the headline "'Is' cannot lead to 'ought.'" I want to show that this headline, which by now has become an all-but-sacred shibboleth in moral philosophy, is extremely confusing, in no way represents the actual argument being made, and should be dropped. But first we must understand the nature of an "ought" statement.

Given the mind's computerlike ability to figure out the meaning of short spoken statements, the "ought" statement must nevertheless push this ability to its very limit. "Ought" statements are certainly among the most elliptic found in language, and their background arguments among the most complex of all background arguments. The background argument involves:

- Two choices: one major, one minor.
- Two "facts": one specific, one general.*
- Two imperatives: one specific, one general.
- A criterion or desire that serves as a guide to action.

The statement that I made to you, my boss, was: "Jones is the wrong man for the job; [therefore] we ought not to hire him." This statement does not actually represent an "is" to "ought"

---

*"Facts" in quotes because in an "ought" statement a "fact" doesn't have to be true for the argument to proceed and lead to a logical conclusion; *all we have to do is to believe it to be true.*

argument, for what we have here is a hybrid ("Jones is the wrong man for the job"). The "ought" phrase is redundant, since it is obvious that we ought not to hire the wrong man for the job. But when you asked me why, I could have given you a true "is" to "ought" statement, namely, "Jones is a two-time embezzler, *therefore* we ought not to hire him." Given only our shared desire not to be fired (to simplify matters), this statement means:

We *must not* hire Jones if we *choose* to keep employed. Keeping employed or not is our *major choice*, and once we have made it in favor of keeping employed, keeping employed is the criterion or desire that serves as our *guide to action*. The *specific fact* is that Jones is a two-time embezzler; the *general fact* is that those who hire a two-time embezzler will, in all probability, be fired. Our *minor choice* is whether to hire Jones or not, but it disappears if we accept the facts and choose to keep employed—then we *must not* hire Jones (we have no choice). This is the *specific imperative*. But my entire statement and its tone are also *like* an imperative. I am not saying "If by chance you choose to keep employed, then you must not hire Jones," but rather "For God's sake, choose continued employment as your guide to action, and therefore don't hire Jones!" This is the *general imperative*. Thus it is that an "ought" statement takes us, by logical progression, from an "is" or a "fact" to a "must," assuming we have chosen a certain criterion or intend to satisfy a certain desire.

When moral questions arise, everything is the same as in the nonmoral use of "ought," with one exception. (I must remind the reader that for now I am putting questions that are generally considered to be moral—e.g., abortion—under the heading of "morality," which is to say that I am following common practice.) If a woman has an unwanted pregnancy and she goes for advice to a priest who says, "Abortion is contrary to the word of God; therefore you ought not to have one," he is taking her from what he believes to be a fact (God said no to abortion) to an "ought" in a perfectly legitimate manner, since we can assume that the woman is there to find out the word of God. Having found it out (and if she believes it), then if she *chooses* to live by the word of God, she *must not* have an abortion. Nor is the priest idly offering the woman a choice, for there is a general imperative expressed by his words; he is saying, "Choose God as your guide!"

The one substantive difference between the Jones and the abortion arguments is *the guide to action*. We can say, "If we hire Jones we will probably be fired, but I see a more important consideration . . ." without being illogical. (There can be more important things in life than not being fired.) But we cannot say, "Abortion is immoral, it is contrary to the word of God, but even more important . . ." without being illogical. For the believer the word of God is morality, it is the ultimate guide to action; there is nothing more important than it. Thus one guide is ultimate while the other is not, and that is the important difference between the two "ought" statements.

Laying out all the elements behind the Jones and the abortion statements, we see a correspondence:

	JONES	*ABORTION*
MAJOR CHOICE	To keep employed or not	To live by the word of God or not
MINOR CHOICE	To hire Jones or not	To have an abortion or not
SPECIFIC FACT (an "is")	Jones is a two-time embezzler	The woman is pregnant
GENERAL FACT (an "is")	Those who hire a two-time embezzler run an obvious risk of being fired*	God said no to abortion
GUIDE TO ACTION	Keeping employed	God

---

*At first glance this fact may seem very different from the (alleged) fact that God said no to abortion. But actually it's the same kind of statement, at least in the sense I employ here. The "voice of business" (if it had a voice) would say no to hiring two-time embezzlers for an accounting job.

SPECIFIC IMPERATIVE (a "must")	Don't hire Jones	Don't have an abortion
GENERAL IMPERATIVE	Choose employment!	Choose God!

"Ought" statements can also be used incorrectly (in a way that deceives and/or confuses the listener), and they frequently are misused by moralists and the clergy—to say, for example, "Abortion is immoral; therefore you ought not to have one." This statement suggests that our (major) choice is whether to be moral or not, and stacks the deck in favor of the speaker's own position, since most of us don't want to be immoral or to be labeled immoral. The real choice, however, is whether or not to accept the criterion from which the moralist has derived the proscription against abortion.

I must say, though, that when I listen to the Reverend Billy Graham on television I am impressed by his fairness when he uses "ought" statements, and by his understanding of all the elements in the background argument. For example, when he argues that we ought not to have sex outside of marriage, he begins with our major choice—namely, whether to live by the word of God and spend eternity in heaven, or to follow the way of the Devil and burn forever. He then urges us to choose God as our guide to action. And finally—going on the assumption that we have chosen God, and desire and intend to live by His word—Reverend Graham lists various things we must not do (including having sex outside of marriage), for, according to him, such acts are contrary to the word of God. There is a grave initial fallacy in Reverend Graham's argument, as we are about to see, but his understanding of "ought" statements seems to me right on the mark. Or, put in other words, his logic after his initial error is precise.

THE NATURAL AND THEOLOGICAL FALLACIES

I said at the opening of the previous section that there is a major argument in modern moral philosophy that has been given the headline "'Is' cannot lead to 'ought,'" and that I have a quarrel with the headline. The quarrel I can settle, at least to my own satisfaction, in a line or two, but it can't be settled without first understanding the major argument. And since that is an argument important to my later argument about morality, let me present it now:

An "is"—God, pleasure, pain, desire, nature, evolution, or any *thing*, natural or supernatural, that exists or that is believed to exist —cannot serve as an ultimate guide to action.* Or, as it is sometimes put, what is *real* cannot tell us what is *good*. And this means, among other things, that an "is" cannot be used to define the basic words of morality—"right" and "wrong," "good" and "bad"—as in "Bad is that which causes greater pain to the greater number," or "Good is that which is in keeping with the word of God."

To attempt to use an "is" as the foundation of morality and to define the basic words in terms of this "is" is, supposedly, to commit either the naturalistic or the theological fallacy—errors first exposed by G. E. Moore when he asked, in effect, "How do you know that what you are defining good in terms of is, itself, necessarily *good*? Or that you have the *right* foundation?"† This kind of question will be asked indefinitely of any *thing* the naturalist or theologian comes up with by way of an answer. For example:

- *The naturalistic fallacy:* Good is that which increases the

---

*Wittgenstein made the is/ought argument dramatically in "Lecture on Ethics," *Philosophical Review*, 64, p. 12. He asked the reader to imagine an omniscient being bent on writing a complete factual account of the universe, listing, that is, every fact there is to know in one book. Such a book, he argued, "would contain nothing that we could call an ethical judgment or anything that would logically imply such a judgment." Facts simply exist and compel nothing but more facts. He went on to say that if someone could truly write a book of ethical judgments derived from the facts, it would "explode and destroy all the other books in the world," for ethics is "supernatural." (Moore argues, as we are about to see, that ethics can't even be supernatural.)

†For Moore's argument see *Principia Ethica* (Cambridge, England: University Press, 1903), chapter one, and pp. 123ff. and 214ff. What I am calling the "theological fallacy" has generally been called the "metaphysical fallacy," but "theological" seems more to the point of those who, by and large, made the actual error, namely, theologians.

amount of pleasure in the world. But how do you know that increasing pleasure is necessarily a good thing? Because all men and women desire pleasure. But how do you know that what all men and women desire is necessarily a good thing? And this kind of question, supposedly, can be asked *ad infinitum* of any *thing* found in nature, such as desire or pleasure, that is proposed as the ultimate good or ultimate guide to action.

• *The theological fallacy:* Assuming we hear a voice from beyond, how do we know that it, itself, is good? Hearing a voice from beyond—or seeing a spectacular being who speaks to us and performs miracles—we would have no idea whatsoever that we were confronting a good being, or whether we should follow its instructions, if we did not have *a prior and independent criterion for judging what was good and right for us to do.* If the voice said, "Go kill all your neighbors," we might well judge, if we were sane, that it was the voice of evil. (And if it said, "You will burn forever in hell if you don't do what I say," we still wouldn't know it was necessarily a good being, only that it was powerful.) All of which is to say that a *voice from beyond cannot be our ultimate guide*—we need something first by which to judge voices, or to judge prophets who have heard voices, or who are, in some other way in touch with spectacular beings. Nor would it matter what this being said about itself or what we believed to be true about it (e.g., that it put our moral awareness in us in the first place)—we would still be led into an endless series of questions.

Thus we are forced to conclude, the argument runs, that *nothing natural or supernatural* can be an ultimate guide to action or serve as the foundation of a list of dos and don'ts, or be used to define good. And, supposedly, we must either turn elsewhere (e.g., to our intuitions) or we must conclude that morality is without rational foundation (the argument of the emotivists).

While I agree that a voice from beyond cannot be the foundation of morality, and will call on Moore's reasoning in subsequent arguments of my own, I am of two minds on the naturalistic fallacy. Like many other philosophers, I have found the critique of naturalism to be an invaluable tool in exposing the errors made by certain philosophers, as well as social Darwinists, sociobiologists, and male chauvinists. *That something is natural does not prove that it is good.*

However, I also believe that Moore and the linguistic philosophers, including Wittgenstein and Bertrand Russell—in teasing their point to its logical limit (that *nothing* natural, i.e., found in nature, can serve as the foundation of morality)—finally got themselves out on a linguistic limb that is easily snapped in the real world of desire. (Indeed, Wittgenstein, Russell, and Moore all came to acknowledge that they were pretty much out on a limb.*) I shall have more to say on this matter in the next chapter, but now I want to settle quickly my immediate quarrel with the linguists, namely, that their headline "'Is' cannot lead to 'ought'" is, at best, extremely confusing.

It is confusing because, as I have tried to show, we go from "is" to "ought" all the time in ordinary and perfectly legitimate discourse. "Ought" statements (which actually take us from "is" to "must") have their humble jobs to do, and they do them countless times each day without problems *when people do share the same criterion or desire.* The end-of-the-line metaethical question "How do you know that what you are using as your ultimate guide to action is, itself, necessarily good?" or "By what criterion have you chosen your criterion?" is a legitimate question, and is in fact central to this book. But if the linguistic philosopher wants to

---

*Toward the end of his life Wittgenstein said he agreed with those who say that "good is what God orders," since it cuts off any rational attempt to explain why something is good or bad (Friedrich Waismann, "Notes on Talks with Wittgenstein." *Philosophical Review*, 74, pp. 12-16). Since Wittgenstein's teaching up to this point indicated no belief in a talking God, we must assume that his remark was meant to be arch, and that he was dismissing the question of morality as being unanswerable. If we take him seriously, then he is guilty of the theological fallacy.

In a footnote added to a reprint of "The Elements of Ethics" (first published in 1910, reprinted in Wilfrid Sellars and John Hospers, eds., *Readings in Ethical Theory*, New York: Appleton-Century-Crofts, 1952, p. 1) Bertrand Russell was in a similar frame of mind, and said he had found it difficult to "work out any satisfactory view of morality" and had "refrained from further writing in the field" of metaethics. As for Moore, he ended up equally exasperated, as we shall see in the next chapter.

say that an "is" cannot serve as the ultimate guide because we can continue to ask "How do you know that your 'is' is the right 'is'?" then let him or her say it, and leave the word "ought" out of any headlines. If a headline is needed for the actual argument that is made by the linguists, then let it be G. J. Marx's famous line, "Whatever it is, I'm against it!"

I want to get to the false hybrid as it is found in nonmoral discourse as quickly as possible. But first let me say a few more words about desires and introduce the concept of "opinion" as I will be using it—all of which is necessary to our understanding of the false hybrid.

DESIRE: THE DEGREE OF COMMONALITY

I want to look at desires—those that require us to say something for their satisfaction or that may require us to say something—from two different angles: how common they are, and how important they are to us. I shall start with the degree of commonality—and while I could as well work with the world at large to make my distinctions, let me continue with the smaller universe that gave us the Jones hybrid, namely, our company. In our company there are desires that everyone or just about everyone has; desires that only some of us have; and (possibly) a desire (relevant to the company) that only one person may have.

The desires that virtually everyone in a group has I will call common desires, and they, in turn, can be divided into three classes:

1. A desire that requires us to work together for its satisfaction, e.g., that our company prosper.

2. A desire that may or may not require us to work together to satisfy, e.g., the desire not to be fired, the desire to be respected by our peers—there are things we can do on our own that will get us fired and cause us to be a laughing stock; on the other hand, if the accounting department doesn't improve its performance you and I may be fired and ridiculed.

3. A desire that puts us all in conflict, that we can't work together to satisfy, and, indeed, that can be satisfied by only one person, e.g., to be company president. This is a common and conflicting desire.

Note: I mentioned desires 1 and 2 before; they are the desires I placed under the heading "shared desire"—and we can now give a shorter definition to this term: namely, any common desire in a group that may require us to work together to satisfy, with the understanding that, by my definition, not only is the desire shared but everyone knows or can assume that nearly everyone else has it (and therefore it doesn't have to be mentioned when we are talking and trying to make a decision).

At the other end of this spectrum is the *singular desire*—a desire that most people in the group don't hold, such as my desire to be fired because I don't have the courage to quit. A *singular and secret desire* (as I will use the term) is one that only one or a few people have, that threatens to frustrate a generally shared desire, and that, if revealed, would at a minimum hurt one's chances of getting what one wanted (for example, I may desire to hire Jones because he has promised me $10,000 if he gets the job).

Between the *common desire* and the *singular desire* there are desires that some hold but some don't. Some want the company to move into electronics, some don't. When the partisans of one side are gathered together they can form hybrids, such as "Thomas is the wrong man for the presidency; he is scared to death of anything to do with electronics."

Needless to say, this particular analysis of desire could be greatly refined, but I think it will get us by, with some further elaborations as they are needed. Let us now approach the phenomenon of desire from another direction.

DESIRE: THE DEGREE OF IMPORTANCE

Most of our actions—which is to say the end product of our desires that see the light of day—are based on desires that are logically derived from higher-order desires. If I must have (and therefore must desire) B to satisfy my desire for A, then A is the higher-order desire and B is the derived desire; and A is the important desire, for if I didn't need B to get A, then B wouldn't be of any importance to me. Thus: I want to get on the bus because I want to get to the train; I want to get to the train because I want to get to the office—all of these desires derived from the higher-order desire to keep my job. A *basic desire*—as I will use the term—is one not immediately or obviously derived from a higher-order desire. When someone asks me why I want to be company president I may say, "I don't know," or "Just because I do," and not choose to discuss or think about the matter any more, in which case being company president is a basic desire as far as I am concerned. It is without justification, although it is not, necessarily, psychologically or philosophically ultimate. Thus it is that we can have several basic desires, for example, to remain alive and healthy, to become president of our company, to have our daughter finish college, etc.—desires that don't ordinarily elicit the question "Why?" We go through life making thousands of decisions involving one or another of our basic desires with no problems raised. On occasion, however, we are faced with a decision that, no matter how it is made, will frustrate one basic desire while satisfying another. (The doctor says, "Either you give up your quest for the presidency or you will ruin your health.") Which is to say that basic desires are not necessarily ultimate; they can be put in conflict, although one of them, upon analysis, could be ultimate—and this is a point I will explore later on. (The question of how an individual chooses among his or her basic desires when they conflict is an interesting one, but I have no answer, nor, fortunately, is an answer important to my argument.)

Now, it may be that someone on the board of directors may ask me why I want to be president, and I hope I will have a more acceptable answer than "I don't know," or "Just because I do," i.e., one that suggests that everyone's desire that the company will prosper will be well served by my promotion, and that service to all is my main motivation. I hope, too, that someone won't ask me why in the world I want to serve people, for here I may stumble badly.* Fortunately, in life, the end of the line is recognized for the bog it is, and most people—other than philosophers and psychiatrists—have the good taste to allow one to get off a few stops before it with some mild and pleasing rhetoric. In any case, my desire to be company president is pretty much a basic desire, and from it, in fact, hundreds of other desires are derived each day.

Before I end this section, let me repeat quickly two observations in light of what I have just been saying. First, the hybrid argument tells us how best to satisfy our shared desires, but it does not judge these desires, and in this regard there are two possibilities: what we want, we should not want according to the generally shared desires of other people (or even one person); or what we want may turn out to be, upon examination, inconsistent with respect to something that is more important to us. (Consider, if you will, the American Olympic athletes in 1980: They all desperately wanted to compete in Moscow, but others didn't want them to go, and some of the athletes didn't want to go either, because their patriotism was more important to them than going.)

My second point: If I have any desire—shared, singular, basic, secret—I may be aware of, or can discover, a *verifiable proposition* relevant to the satisfaction of my desire. (If I desire to burn down company headquarters, there are books filled with verified propositions about inflammables that can be helpful to me.) Furthermore, there are usually things I must say to achieve my goal. ("Let me have twenty gallons of gasoline in these cans, please.")

---

*During the 1980 primaries Senator Edward Kennedy was taken by surprise in a television interview when Roger Mudd asked him why he wanted to be President. For one dreadful minute—that would plague him for weeks afterward—Kennedy mumbled incoherently. He probably sensed he could not say "Because I think it would be neat living in the White House" or "Making President is the name of the game," but, taken by surprise by this end-of-the-line question, he was at a loss for one of those generally acceptable—if usually meaningless—answers that must flow from ambitious men and women like treacle, e.g., "To meet the great challenge facing our country," which begs the question "Why in the world do you want to meet great challenges?" (But this is not a question asked in polite society, and would probably not have been asked by Mr. Mudd.)

And there are things I may say—all toward satisfying my goal. (To the company president, "A nightwatchman is unnecessary—a needless expense in this neighborhood.") *However*, unless our intention is to deceive or confuse, *there is only one instance* in which a desire permits us to drop personal pronouns, omit the desire, and speak in the objective grammatical form—and that is when we have good reason to believe the other person or persons have the desire *and* when we have a verifiable proposition relevant to satisfying the desire. Then we have the hybrid. To use the hybrid form at any other time is confusing and often infuriating, as we shall see in our discussion of the false hybrid.*

OPINION

The computerlike ability of the brain enables us to detect truth in the hybrid statement, even though we are not consciously aware of the compelling background argument. This "computer," when it is working well, can also give us a feel that we don't have the elements necessary to form a hybrid, and if this is the case and if it is not our intention to deceive or confuse, then we must employ a nonhybrid way of talking. The easiest way to do this— and to avoid long or cumbersome explanations—is to insert the word "opinion" or "judgment" in our statement. This has the dramatic effect of changing the whole tone of our argument; of cutting the force of the hybrid by half, at least; and of removing the question from the area of truth. Thus in the case of another candidate for the accounting job, I might say, *"In my opinion* Boozer is the wrong man for the job." Expanded, my argument might run as follows:

"Given our shared desires and the facts I have been able to gather about Boozer, I am aware of no verifiable proposition relevant to these facts that will give us a clear indication that our

---

*There is always the possibility of what might be called the "empathetic hybrid"— the speaker is not involved in the decision to be made (e.g., he's not in our company), but he doesn't want to see us fired and so he says, "Jones is the wrong man for the job."

desires will be satisfied or frustrated if we hire him. Nevertheless, he was fired from his last job for what he claims was a 'personality clash'; is three times divorced; had three martinis at lunch; and never looked me in the eye during our interview, and I am using these admittedly uncertain guides to the future performance of individuals as my criteria, and have formed the opinion that he won't satisfy our desires as well as one of the other candidates."

This is to say that in uncertain situations only an uncertain statement will do—always assuming our intention is not to deceive, confuse, or infuriate—and introducing the word "opinion" or "judgment" signals to the listener(s) this uncertainty.

Some observations on the Boozer opinion, and opinions in general:

• The great change in meaning that occurs when we insert the word "opinion" in a statement is not a magic trick. It is quickly explained by reference to the dictionary—"Opinion . . . a belief less strong than positive knowledge."* However, once we appreciate the nature of hybrids, I believe we can give a simple, but more precise definiton to opinion—this often difficult and elusive concept—namely: "A statement that lacks certain essential elements of a hybrid."

As for the word "judgment," I would do as the dictionary does and define it in terms of opinion—"the process of forming an opinion or evaluation by discerning and comparing." Or, in other words, an opinion that some work has gone into, including the training of the person offering it.

• How an individual actually forms opinion is a question over which there has been considerable debate among psychologists and to which I have nothing to add. My point is only that in decision-making situations there may be truth based on a shared

---

*All dictionary definitions that I will use are from *Webster's New Collegiate Dictionary* (Springfield, Mass.: Merriam-Webster, 1975). The discussion here and throughout the book is about opinion related to decisions we must make about a *course of action*, and not questions of aesthetics or personal taste.

desire and a verifiable proposition (e.g., the hybrid: given the truth of what happened in the past, *this decision* holds the best possible chance of satisfying the desire), or if there are not the makings of truth, then we must form opinion. That we may think our opinion is truth is a very common phenomenon; that we cannot *consciously* form opinion unless we first recognize that we are in the area of opinion is also true. But the major point of my argument is this: Which area we are in can be determined objectively, by going to the background argument of the statement made and seeing if we have all the elements necessary to form a hybrid—if we don't, then we are in the area of opinion, regardless of where we may think we are. In short, if there is no obvious "best possible decision" but we must reach a decision, then we must take a chance; go with our gut feeling; form an opinion—for even if we are traumatized and cannot act, that, too, is a decision.

• While the statement "In my opinion Boozer is the wrong man for the job" looks as if it might be of the order of "In my opinion, Columbus, the world is flat" (an opinion about something unknown at the moment, but verifiable in principle), most of the time, in ordinary discourse about a decision to be made, slipping in the word "opinion" or "judgment" has the deflating effect of saying that the situation is hopelessly unverifiable. Many background elements in the Boozer statement might be confirmed, verified, or quantified, but even if they were (for example, to show that those who drink three martinis at lunch run a 6 percent chance of becoming dysfunctional alcoholics within the next five years) it is unlikely that they would lead to an *obvious and unacceptable risk* for most business people; we would still have to *make a judgment* between two courses of action (to hire or not hire Boozer) neither of which is obviously dangerous or clearly satisfying to almost everyone. Sensing this—and seeing no profit or loss in it for me whether or not Boozer is hired—I put my case in the form of an opinion lest the listener think that I thought Boozer was, like Jones, *clearly the wrong man for the job.* In other words my "computer" alerted me to the fact that with Boozer I didn't have the makings of a hybrid, and I slipped comfortably into an alternative, nonobjective way of talking.

• Given what I will call "enormous numbers," opinions can become hybrids. If we discovered, for example, that Boozer usually has nine martinis at lunch and was restraining himself with me, we would then have a hybrid, namely, "Boozer is the wrong man for the job!"—a true statement given the verifiable proposition that anyone who has nine martinis in an hour will be drunk, and given our shared desire not to have a drunk on our hands every afternoon. At what martini we actually get a drunk depends on the individual, but that it is well passed, by all, at the ninth martini seems indisputable. "Enormous numbers" are important to our understanding of what passes for morality, for a lot of what passes for morality is founded on *fear* of "enormous numbers" (if everyone had sex only with those of the same sex that would be the end of the world), and my point will be that "enormous numbers" themselves and *fear* of "enormous numbers" are two different things.

• In any particular group there are usually those who are wiser than others when it comes to forming opinion, those with a better track record than others at predicting the results of a decision from less-than-compelling evidence. And there are usually fools as well—those with an uncanny knack for coming up with the opinion that more often than not leads to disaster. Often, however, the most important contribution the wise person makes to the group is his or her instinctive understanding of the difference between the hybrid and opinion, and pointing out in a heated argument that truth is not at issue and that those who think it is are not only mistaken but dangerous, since their brains are short-circuiting. (Not, of course, that the wise person puts it this way.) That the passionate are innocent in their misuse of the hybrid form and in their belief that truth is at stake makes them all the more dangerous, since they know, deep down, that their motives are pure, and therefore believe that everyone in disagreement with them must be guilty and impure. But I am running ahead of myself; for now let us just leave it that some people are more gifted than others at predicting the results of a decision.

TESTING FOR HYBRIDS

The line between a hybrid and an opinion may be unclear at times (in which case we probably don't have a hybrid), but it is, I hope, also true that there is a line beyond which almost everyone (with the same desire) will recognize opinion or the hybrid—as I have defined the terms. Jones *is* the wrong man for the job (in an elliptic manner of speaking); Boozer is neither right nor wrong given the evidence available. In one case we have come to a fork in the road, and the signs are clear; in the other case we have come to a traffic circle, with many confusing signs. But in any case, if we are getting static, speaker to listener, we can trouble-shoot it by going to the background argument and looking for the various elements that are required to form a hybrid. If we do this, then at least we will know where our true differences lie, and not be sucked into a whirlwind of confused and accusing words.

There are two quick tests that can help determine whether we have a hybrid or an opinion. First, when we hear the word "wrong," for example, we can ask, "Wrong in terms of what?" and this will usually turn up a desire or criterion; if it is not generally shared, then we don't have an essential ingredient of the hybrid—and there is other work to be done before we can decide on the question we face. On the other hand, this method can also turn up the fact that we do indeed have the makings of a hybrid, and the person resisting its truth is out in left field—he or she simply doesn't share the desire of everyone else in the group. If we ask, "Wrong in terms of what?" and the speaker replies, "Not wrong in terms of anything, just wrong in and of itself," or, "I just have a gut feeling it is wrong," then this is an argument from intuition, and while it may be worth considering when all else fails, it is opinion and clearly not the stuff of hybrids.

The second test for determining whether we have a hybrid or an opinion is to add the word "opinion" to whatever statement is being made. *If the result sounds odd and jarring,* then the statement is probably a true hybrid, for the "computer" rebels at any truth put in the opinion form. For example, "In *my opinion* arsenic is a poison" sounds odd and jarring. And so, too, does "In *my opinion* Jones is the wrong man for the job." Arsenic and two-time embezzlers are not matters of opinion. But if I say, "In *my opinion* Boozer is the wrong man for the job," the statement has a proper ring, given the less-than-compelling evidence available on the man. A general rule of thumb that can become second nature is: When you are seriously thinking about anything, *always* slip in the word "opinion" before the statement you are about to make, and take it out only when the resulting statement sounds truly ridiculous— if your intention is not to bewitch or to be bewitched by the sound of your own words. This has the effect of correcting any short-circuiting in the brain; and changes how we think by (purposely) changing how we talk. For example, if we take some precious belief of ours that is actually an opinion and not a hybrid or other truth and put the words "in my opinion" in front of it, and if we repeat the new phrase to ourselves several hundred or even several thousand times, we may, I believe, radically change our attitude toward our belief and toward those who don't hold it. I will expand on this point as we go along, but I might just add now that I have done this with my own most precious beliefs (that are, in fact, opinions) and there is no doubt that I am not the man I used to be.

THE FALSE HYBRID

The statement "Boozer is the wrong man for the job" is a false hybrid. It looks just like a hybrid, but when we go to the background argument we find we don't have the elements necessary to form a hybrid and are less than certain as to what to do. The "computer" may well alert us to this uncertainty and if we have no axe to grind or a game to play we may well signal our uncertainty on Boozer by placing the word "opinion" in front of our statement. However, the word "opinion" signals uncertainty to such a degree that opinion has a generally low reputation alongside of truth, and I cannot deny that a "vigorous game player" can often improve his or her chances for advancement by using the bold hybrid form to express opinions, saying, for example, "Boozer is the *right* man for the job!" and winning a reputation for tough-mindedness that may serve him or her well even after the decision proves disastrous.

There is, however, a big difference between the deceptions practiced by a skilled game player and the self-deception caused by one's failure to appreciate the difference between the hybrid and the false hybrid. When we have formed a serious opinion about a course of action to be taken, we also have a desire, namely, that our opinion prevail. Since we now have a combination of two things, neither of which is much respected (opinion and desire), we may instinctively grasp for objective support (nothing is more respected than truth) and come up with the false hybrid. It is often true that within moments of making our statement we are in a heated argument out of all proportion to the importance of the decision at hand, and the fault, we say, is not ours but the other person's for denying the truth—or so it seems.

Thus if Bill—holding the generally shared desires of everyone else in the company; having no secret and singular desire with regard to Boozer's hiring; and having the same information that I have, but *feeling strongly that he should not be hired*—puts his opinion in the bold hybrid form and says, "Boozer is the wrong man for the job!" he—unlike the skilled game player who instinctively knows what he or she is up to and knows when to back off—may well believe his statement to be true, since the more he says it, the truer it sounds, reflecting as it does his deepest convictions on the matter. Now if someone says to him, "Well, that's your opinion," and follows it up with, "Let's face it, Bill, you just don't want to hire Boozer," Bill may become unhinged—as he would if a true statement were contradicted and personal motivations raised—and scream, "It's not a matter of opinion! It has nothing to do with what I want!"

The jolt of truth that Bill and all of us get when we use the hybrid form correctly—the *certainty* that Jones is the wrong man for the job—Bill also feels when he unknowingly employs the powerful hybrid form to express himself regarding Boozer. What Bill is saying not only sounds identical to a hybrid, it feels identical and looks identical (when written out). There are fewer things in life more difficult than recognizing when we are talking opinion on matters that are important to us, for the simple reason that, language and the brain being as they are, we don't see, believe, or feel that we are.

But what is important to us is often the result of *how we talk*—and the reaction we get. After all, it is probably not that important to Bill that Boozer not be hired, or even that his opinion prevail; but what is vital to Bill—and to all of us—is that he be taken seriously and that his motivation not be impugned. This Bill has unwittingly invited by using the hybrid form to express himself on Boozer. One of Bill's associates—the speaker above—has, in trying to expose Bill's error without himself actually understanding it, raised the question of Bill's integrity ("Let's face it, Bill . . ."—*it* being, supposedly, what is really on Bill's mind) and driven him wild, for Bill knows, *with absolute certainty*, that he had no intention of deceiving anyone. From here the argument easily gets out of hand, for Bill is *absolutely right* (he wasn't trying to deceive anyone), and his associate is also *absolutely right*—the Boozer question is a matter of opinion and not truth.

Where there is truth—or where there is something *perceived to be true*—anger is never far away if we are contradicted. I believe the reason for this is twofold: (1) It is disorienting; we suddenly fear we may be losing our minds. If I know it is Tuesday and someone insists it is Wednesday, either he is wrong or I am mad, and so I scream my affirmation of the truth, "It's Tuesday, you idiot, wake up, pull yourself together, get hold of yourself!"— actually expressing my own fears if he turns out to be right. (2) We can be in real danger when those we are dealing with believe something to be true that is not true, and by our anger we try to force the truth on them: "For God's sake, wake up, the gas tank is near *empty*, land the plane at *that* airport immediately!" My point is that we become equally angry when we think we are talking truth but are not.

"ALEXANDER IS THE WRONG MAN FOR THE JOB"

The false hybrid can also be used to deceive, in which case we don't have an opinion masquerading as truth, but simply a lie. I can say, for example, "Alexander is the wrong man for the job; we ought not to hire him," by which I mean, were all elements uncovered, "I don't like him," or "I don't like those in the company who are pushing his candidacy," or "I think he is such an excellent candidate that I fear he will get the promotion I am in line for." Despite appearances, my statement on Alexander is a false hybrid.

But just as with Bill, if I repeat my statement on Alexander often enough to myself and others, I may come to believe it is true, since it sounds so true, being, as it is, in perfect harmony with my deepest emotions. And I may become equally angry if someone contradicts me—not just giving vent to my true emotions (dislike or fear of Alexander) but because, as I have just noted, we often become angry when truth (and by extension perceived truth) is contradicted.

Admittedly, you—the boss—may ask the reasons for my statement on Alexander, and while I certainly won't give you my real reasons (and may no longer recognize them), and while the phony reasons I do give may be offered as nothing more than vague intuitions ("Just something about the man . . ."), you, busy as you are, may be only half paying attention once I get beyond "Alexander is the wrong man for the job," and—recalling that I had said the same thing about Jones—may nod and move on to the next candidate. The important point here is that when I say "Alexander is the wrong man for the job," your reaction is not, "Oh, you don't like him," or "Oh, you fear him," but one of credence; what I am saying *could be true*, and because you are busy, and because you trust me, you (too quickly) accept it as true.

If word gets back to you that Alexander is an excellent candidate* and and you call me to your office for an explanation, and if

---

*Generally speaking, as I have noted, it is easier to recognize a road to disaster than to find the road to success. Because there are wrong men and women for a job, it does not necessarily follow that there is a right man or woman for the job in the hybrid sense. It all depends on what we want and what reliable tests or verifiable propositions are available against which to measure candidates and predict the probable outcome if they are hired. But let us assume, for the sake of argument, when a candidate is respected by his boss and peers (we could take a poll), and when the job move is lateral, although for more money, that such candidates have an excellent chance of being respected for their work in the new

I have not been carried too far from reality by the sound of my own words, and know enough to know that I may be in trouble, I can probably weasel out by saying, "Well look, it was my opinion. I have nothing personal against the man . . ." and sufficiently muddy the waters to avoid serious trouble. But if the hybrid and the false hybrid were generally recognized for what they are, you would then be able to nail me as no "vigorous game player" or liar has ever been nailed before, namely: "In serious discussions with me on *any* decision we have to make, *never* use the hybrid form when it is not supported by a full hybrid argument, or I will terminate you on the spot as a grammatical illiterate, or a liar."

HIDDEN DEFINITIONS

Most often when we misuse the hybrid form, it is not our intention to deceive. Nevertheless, any misuse creates a lot of trouble. Indeed, I would say that half the arguments in life are exacerbated by the unintentional misuse of the hybrid form and the listener's frustration at not being able to name the actual error being made. The hybrid communicates vast amounts of truth in ordinary, rapid-fire discourse. The false hybrid communicates (and hides) vast amounts of opinion and emotion. But since the two statements are identical in form and call on identical words ("right," "wrong," "good," "bad"), and neither is recognized for what it is, we find ourselves in a world where everyone is waving red flags at one another, and sometimes the flags mean real danger to a shared desire, and sometimes they mean "I want this" or "Some of us want this." The point is that a red flag, which can mean danger to us all, cannot be used any way we like—without confusion and peril.

Nor have linguistic philosophers been any help in clarifying

---

job—and that Alexander is such a candidate. That Alexander may prove to be a disaster is irrelevant to this point, for (as always) we are dealing with probabilities, and in this case no one can fault us for hiring him—even though someone probably will if he proves to be a disaster.

matters. Indeed, one school—the philosophers of Ordinary Language*—has, it seems to me, gone out of its way to further confuse matters. These philosophers, following the lead of Wittgenstein in *Philosophical Investigations*,† argue that such words as "right" and "wrong," "good" and "bad" (in and out of morality) *have many meanings* ("linguistic pluralism") and that it has been a grave error of philosophers (and in particular moral philosophers) to try to find one meaning or essence. Wittgenstein said, "The meaning of a word is its use in language" (section 43). And in a widely cited example using the word "game," he showed that there are many activities that are called games but that have little if anything in common (e.g., solitaire and soccer). Which is to say that no one definition of the word "game" exists that includes all the activities that are called "games" (sections 66, 67).

This is all very well, but when we go to common usage we also discover that there are other kinds of words (pencil, pear, arsenic) that neatly and exclusively define certain things, *which is to say they have quite precise definitions.*‡ Now, I do not know what limits, if any, Wittgenstein would establish for the use of words *without* precise definitions (and indeed the word "game" seems to be one of those words that today, even more than when Wittgenstein was writing, people use to cover just about any activity), but clearly we cannot use words *with* precise definitions any way we like without confusion and even extreme danger. A meat cleaver is not a

---

*The founder of this school is Wittgenstein, but among those who carried out his work in the area of morality are Stephen Toulmin, Stuart Hampshire, Margaret Macdonald, J. L. Austin, and R. M. Hare. One way or another, these philosophers argue that the basic terms of morality do not have precise definitions. I will argue just the opposite, and that the failure to appreciate these precise definitions has led to much of the confusion surrounding the nature of morality.

†Ludwig Wittgenstein, *Philosophical Investigations*, translated by G. E. M. Anscombe, (Oxford, England: Blackwell, 1953).

‡A word can have two or more precise definitions, but if it does, *then the context in which the word is used must indicate which definition the speaker has in mind*—if there is not to be confusion. Baseball is a game with nine players on each side, etc., and it is also the ball used to play the game, but invariably the context indicates which definition the speaker has in mind.

scalpel, and if we want one we cannot ask for the other; mistakes like this happen on occasion, and they are rightly called the misuse of words. Futhermore, if we want to use a word with a precise definition in a special or metaphorical way, we must give a linguistic clue to our special or metaphorical use of the word. We cannot say "Wilson is a butcher," if he is not a butcher, without inviting confusion in the minds of people who don't know Wilson. But we can say "Dr. Wilson is a butcher" and get our opinion of his competency across, since the title "doctor" gives a clue to our meaning. If we fail to announce our metaphor when we are using a word with a precise definition, then we are misusing the word against a benchmark of coherence. (The false hybrid is a prime example of the unannounced metaphor, as we are about to see.)

So we get the meaning of a word by going to common usage, but there is such a thing as misusage. Here, then, is my point: There is a small group of words ("morality" and "immorality," "right" and "wrong," "good" and "bad"—the latter four when they are used in both moral and nonmoral decision-making situations) that are extremely peculiar in that they have quite precise definitions in common usage (and are used in accord with their precise definitions countless times each day, specifically in hybrid statements) but are also constantly being misused. By "misused" I mean they are being used in some other sense than their precise definitions, with no linguistic clue given to this other sense. The result is the same as with any misuse of words having precise definitions, namely, confusion. Only in the case of these peculiar words is the misusage so common and the amount of confusion so great that the precise definitions are not apparent. Which is to say these words have "hidden and precise definitions," or, simply, "hidden definitions." (A word with a hidden definition is not unlike a suitcase with a gyroscope in it—as long as we are taking it in the direction it wants to go, there are no problems, but when we try to take it where it doesn't want to go, there is trouble.)

I am a long way from being able to explain why I include "morality" and "immorality" among these words, but let me, for now, concentrate on the word "wrong" as it is used in nonmoral discourse. When we go to the background argument of the common hybrid statement, we discover that the word "wrong" has a precise definition, namely, incorrect and incoherent *of us* to do given a shared desire and verifiable proposition. That this precise definition is not generally recognized does not matter—the precise definition is there, in common usage, and the word is used according to its precise definition countless times each day and it helps to get a tremendous amount of work done smoothly and efficiently. It is, therefore, a word with a precise but hidden definition. Furthermore, it is what might be called a "red flag word"—a word that can signal danger to a shared desire. In the statement "Jones is the wrong man for the job," "wrong" was used according to its precise definition, and there was, consequently, no trouble when I made the statement. But when Bill said, "Boozer is the wrong man for the job," there was all sorts of trouble, including the charge that he was being deceitful.

When the word "wrong" is used in a decision-making situation but not according to its precise definition—in other words, when it is being used metaphorically and therefore represents no *clear and present danger to a shared desire*—then we must give a linguistic clue that the word is being used metaphorically. For example, we can put the word "wrong" in quotation marks or change our inflection, but the best clue is to add the word "opinion" or "judgment" to our statement. Thus when I say, "In my opinion Boozer is the wrong man for the job," I am saying, in effect, "We are not in the realm of the verifiable and Boozer is certainly not in the Jones category, but he may be the wrong man for the job, as I see things, and I have some reasons, but admittedly they are less than compelling, and maybe he will work out, but I tend to think not, and to think that some of our shared desires may be frustrated." By slipping in the word "opinion" I announce my metaphorical use of the word "wrong"—a word that I simply cannot do as I like with because it does have a precise definition.

Now the question arises: Why can't we say that the word "game" does have a precise definition but that people are constantly misusing it, or that the word "wrong" has many definitions (in decision-making situations). Ultimately the answer is the trouble the word is causing. The word "game" doesn't cause much trouble when people use it any way they like because people generally understand what they are doing—"Oh you know what I mean, its like a game." Its constant metaphorical usage has washed out its precise definition. But this isn't true with the word "wrong" where people don't sense what they are doing; where the word is constantly being used according to a precise definition; and where there is constant trouble when the word is not used according to its precise definition. I cannot impose a precise definition on the word "game" because no one will accept it, but I can, I hope, get people to agree with me that the word "wrong" does have a precise definition and that the trouble the word often causes is caused by using the word when its precise definition does not apply.

THE BASIC RULE

The preceding argument can be formulated as a rule: If a word has a precise definiton, then we cannot use the word when its precise definition does not apply, unless we give a linguistic clue to its special or metaphorical usage—if our intention is not to deceive, confuse, or infuriate. (I will call this the Basic Rule.)

While Wittgenstein and his followers would probably have no argument with this Basic Rule (just as I have no argument with them that the word "game" does not have a precise definition), what they failed to appreciate is that such words as "right" and "wrong" do, in fact, have precise definitions when used in decision-making situations. *Therefore,* they fall under the Basic Rule, and, therefore, the fact that these words are constantly used in violation of the Basic Rule means not that they are like the word "game" (i.e., without precise definition) but simply that they are being misused—and we can expect confusion. Indeed, we find tremendous confusion when these words are used in ordinary discourse *because* they are being used in violation of the Basic Rule (nowhere more so than in the case of moral discourse, as we shall see).

Let me end this chapter with some slightly more complex hybrids and false hybrids (although it won't take me as long to explain them now that the basic work has been done), and in doing so turn to the words "good" and "bad," for they, too, as I have said, have precise definitions when found in hybrids.

"IT'S A BEAUTIFUL DAY"

We have seen that adjectives may modify nouns different in the extended argument from those they modify in the spoken hybrid. To further complicate matters—and maybe I had better go immediately to an example—we may be in possession of information such that we can legitimately say the chance of something happening is not only favorable: it is "super-good," "near 100 percent" "perfect," "beautiful," etc. The result of this is that we can find extremely "soft" words such as "beautiful" in a legitimate hybrid, although such a word gives a decidedly nonverifiable look to the spoken statement, and we enter the land of confusion by another road—everyone *knows* that *any* statement with "beautiful" in it is, at best, a matter of opinion.

But everyone is wrong. For example, "It's a beautiful day" may be a hybrid. It may mean: "Given our desire to hold a picnic today, and given the weather conditions and the prediction for today, there is a super-favorable (i.e., beautiful) chance that everyone will turn out for the picnic, for it is verifiable and true that on days similar to this, just about everyone who had made plans to go on a picnic, went."

If this is what I mean, then clearly "beautiful" doesn't modify "day" in the extended argument, but rather the chance that something favorable will occur; and my statement is neither an opinion nor an aesthetic judgment. I could be wrong, but the point is that I could be right, not that everyone will turn out, but that on days similar to this almost everyone has.

On this kind of day, if you and I are responsible for organizing a picnic, there is probably no more precise or efficient way for me to get you up and about your many tasks than to call you and say, "Wake up, let's get started, it's a beautiful day." To give you the actual weather report would be to waste valuable time, and to hedge in any manner—to say "In my opinion it's a beautiful day"—would be to throw you off, and raise questions that would waste even more time if I answered them.

What kind of day it is, is a matter of fact (no clouds, 78 degrees, one-to-three-miles-per-hour winds, etc.), and our shared desire is the key to understanding "beautiful" in this situation, for it is, in truth, a terrible day for those who plan to go ice skating on the pond. We could spend a lifetime trying to define "beautiful" and never come to an agreement, but in this case, once we go to the extended argument, the definition is quickly apparent.

There are also terrible days—days on which only a fool would attempt to have a picnic and not one person in a thousand would show up. (The chance of anyone showing up would be terrible.) And there are pretty good days, and pretty bad days—days on which past experience would indicate that fewer people wanted to go on a picnic, but some people still wanted to go.

AL AND MARY

Let us assume that it is clear and warm, but windy, and that on days similar to this, 15 percent of those who planned to go on a picnic decided not to go because of the wind. Or, put in its elliptic form, "It's a pretty good day," assuming, as I do, that most people would agree to call an 85 percent turnout pretty good. Al and Mary have both made plans to go on their office picnic, and while Al still wants to go, Mary is among the 15 percent who have been turned off by the wind. Theoretically, there is nothing to argue about. Al is in a substantial majority, but Mary is in a respectable minority—hardly a "capricious odd-ball," as he later calls her.

But such is our reluctance to say what it is we want—indeed, our apparent inability to find words to say what we want that don't make us sound crude and selfish—that, instinctively, we grasp for objective support and employ the false hybrid. Mary says, in all innocence, "It's a terrible day," a statement that, if *it were true,* and *it could be,* would fully justify her not wanting to go on the picnic, since only fools want to go on picnics on days when the weather is such that no one else turns up.

Al is annoyed with Mary for not wanting to go, but her statement makes him furious, for he senses it is untrue (and he is right), and that if she is not calling him a fool as such, she is seriously questioning his good sense. But he cannot name her error and so is angry and confused and *makes the same kind of error himself*, countering her claim with: "It's a beautiful day; you just don't want to go on the picnic." And so the battle is joined, for despite the apparent blandness and objectivity of Al's words, Mary is now the one who is infuriated, for she perceives his statement as a personal attack—one accusing her of an unsupported raw wanting, raising questions about her sensitivity to the desires of others, and suggesting character flaws so deep as to be beyond analysis or help. *If it were a beautiful day* then she would either be one of those dreadful neurotics who find fault where no one else finds fault, or she would have capriciously changed her mind in complete disregard of the plans they had made. Or she might be everything—neurotic, capricious, and insensitive.

The basic conflicts of wantings, though they weren't that important in the first place, have now escalated to a major war by the way Al and Mary have expressed themselves. It is a war that must be won, or at least not surrendered, for matters of character have—inadvertently—been raised.

At this point, an elderly gentleman—an old Logical Positivist—steps into the argument and says, " 'It's a beautiful day,' means only that 'I want to go on the picnic.' " While Al and Mary are confused, they are not *that* confused, and for a few moments they unite and heap abuse on the old man and the frightening relativism of his position. Since they can't isolate his monumental error (as we have seen, "It's a beautiful day" can mean a lot more than "I want to go on the picnic"), he only smiles, as he has been doing for years, and moves on, and Al and Mary return to their argument.

If Al and Mary could suddenly realize that it is, *in truth*, a pretty good day, their argument would quickly collapse. On pretty good days some, by definition, are turned off by the weather, and Mary happens to be among them. It's nobody's fault, and there is nothing to argue about. Perhaps they can flip a coin, or go their own ways and plan to meet later on, or one can change his or her mind happily, Al happy that Mary is one of those healthy-minded individuals who don't suffer through unpleasant situations for fear of offending, or Mary happy that Al is with the majority, unlike the minorities of one she usually goes out with. But miracles seldom happen in the real world, where the hybrid is not recognized for what it is, and minor differences are often fanned to fury by the way we talk.

"A BAD CHILD"

Early in life we learn to use the false hybrid to bewitch others, but in the process we often become bewitched ourselves—we learn a trick without understanding it and become furious with our audience when the trick fails to work. The child learns not to come home and say to his parents, "I hate Tommy and wish he was dead because he is so popular." This would only bring a lecture from his parents; instead he says, "Tommy is a bad child," sending a chill through them.

Nor are his parents reassured when they ask, "Why?" and their son furrows his brow and says, "Just because he is." Now, quite concerned, they tell him not to play with Tommy, and the boy leaves in triumph to tell the other children his parents' instructions, humming to himself as he goes, "Tommy is a bad child, Tommy is a bad child," the phrase sounding truer and truer the more he says it, being, as it is, in perfect harmony with his deepest emotions.

His parents, in making inquiries, cause Tommy to come under suspicion, and for a time his popularity actually does dip. What the parents instinctively understand, and what the Logical Positivists ignored, is that their son's statement could be pregnant with terrible truth—"as true as any statement ever made!" *It could be a hybrid!* Expanded, it could mean: "Given our shared desire not to meet a fiery death, and given the verifiable proposition that children playing with matches and kerosene cause many more explosions than those trained in the use of these materials, and given the fact that Tommy is storing kerosene and matches in the basement, there is now a 'bad' risk that our desire will be frustrated."

But fortunately, as we know, the son's statement was an

emotive in the hybrid form, which is to say it was a false hybrid, and in the long run, at least in this case, it is the son who suffers most. Because he failed to understand the trick he played, he believes that he is innocent and that Tommy truly is a bad child, and that everyone is blind to the truth, and the son stews in his own juices, mad at the world. (All this could have been avoided if only his mother or father had said: "Those who use the bold hybrid form when there is no hybrid argument behind it are either liars or grammatical illiterates, so either fill in the background argument or go to your room without dinner.")

In summary, then, a hybrid statement occurs in decision-making situations involving two or more people. It is an elliptic statement with a complex background argument behind it—an argument that leads to the right decision, the decision that (based on evidence from the past) holds the best possibility of satisfying a desire shared by the speaker and the listener. The hybrid is in the objective grammatical form, and it deserves to be, for while it is different from the statements found in science, it is, like them, verifiable—it provides the *best chance* of satisfying the shared desire.

There is also the false hybrid—a statement that looks identical in form to the hybrid (and often employs words typically found in hybrids, such as "right" and "wrong," "good" and "bad") but doesn't have the compelling argument of the hybrid behind it. Such statements often lead to a sense of being deceived on the part of the listener—and to confusion and anger, often out of all proportion to the question or decision we face.

With the hybrid and the false hybrid in hand, let us now turn to morality.

Chapter Two

The Primary Code

There are, I believe, two substantively different things that pass under the heading of morality. One is a set of hybrids, the other is a set of opinions; I will call them, respectively, the primary code and the secondary code. The failure to recognize the difference between these two codes is the great error of moral philosophy.

In morality—or what passes for morality—we have examples of all the errors and problems that we found in nonmoral discourse, including the employment of the hybrid form when it doesn't apply; the unannounced mataphor; the failure to appreciate the hidden definitions of certain words; the violation of the Basic Rule; and the innocent driven wild by what they hear and the reaction to what they say. In broad terms, the great error of moral philosophy has been caused by using the same words and grammatical forms in discussing two very different types of acts, thus creating an illusion of sameness where none, in fact, exists. I am going to try to show that despite appearances, the statements "Murder is wrong" and "Abortion is wrong" are as different as day from night.

THE PRIMARY CODE

Murder *is* wrong—and so are robbery, arson, assault, and pol-

73

lution.* These statements are hybrids, elliptic in the extreme, but ultimately founded on the generally shared desire to stay alive. Expanded, the background argument of these hybrids would run as follows:

Given the generally shared desire to stay alive, it is true and verifiable that our chances are greatly improved in a group rather than alone in the jungle or on the plain. (Man is among those animals least able to survive on his own—at least without goods and implements produced by others. And while man did not consciously choose to live in a group—evolution put him there—the dangers of not remaining in a group have always been obvious enough.)

But there can be no group unless certain acts (murder, arson, etc.) are proscribed and violators segregated or otherwise incapacitated from repeating these acts. If every time we go out the chances are good that we will be killed or mugged, or our loved ones robbed, kidnapped, raped, or otherwise assaulted—then, if *nothing* happens to the person or persons committing these acts, we (and others) will (1) flee, and the group will be destroyed and its potential for helping to keep us alive will be lost; (2) remain and be killed; (3) die, as we are unable to go about the tasks necessary to stay alive. (Robbing, kidnapping, torching, assault, and pollution are not far from killing if what is taken or ruined is necessary to live, such as food, water, clothing, one's dwelling, one's parents, or the use of one's arms and legs.)

---

*These words, "murder," "assault," "robbery," etc., carry heavy moral connotations, and we could spend a lifetime trying to decide whether *this* particular act is *really* robbery, murder, etc. Thus for the purposes of this discussion I ask the reader to place himself or herself on a dark, lonely street with strange noises coming out of even darker alleyways, and then bring to mind the things the reader does not want to happen before he or she arrives home. Let what the reader desperately hopes won't happen (a knife in the back, a blow to the head) serve as prototype "definitions" of the acts covered by such words as "murder," "robbery," "assault," and so forth (with kidnapping, rape, and forced sodomy falling under the heading of assault).

Pollution is obviously a very broad concept; for my purposes let it be an act that leaves the environment different from what it was before *and that creates an immediate threat to life and the group.* Even in the most isolated tribe with a vast environment at its disposal, there is some kind of pollution that is an immediate threat to life and the group, e.g., feces disposal and contamination of the water supply.

If those fleeing finally settle down and form a new group, *then these same acts must be proscribed and violators segregated or otherwise punished,* or this group, too, will break up or be destroyed. If there is no place to flee (as there is none for most of us in today's world), then the mayhem will continue until the last man or woman is killed, or until protective subgroups are formed—but again, *there can be no groups of any kind* unless certain acts are proscribed and violators punished. These proscriptions I will call the primary code—or PC.

Some words of explanation and observations on the primary code:

• I am not saying that a group would be destroyed if everyone were inclined to kill, torch, and rob, for while this is certainly true, there is no evidence that everyone (as earliest hominid or present man) has been so inclined, or that it is the primary code that holds a Hobbesian beast in all of us under constant control.* On the other hand, we cannot ignore the hard evidence that the PC proscriptions and punishments do act as a deterrent—for example, the large amount of violent crime that often occurs after a major disaster or during a blackout when the police are not present, or when, in effect, some people feel free to violate the PC restrictions. But I am arguing now that if *one person* and only one person were allowed to commit certain acts freely, this would in all probability destroy the group as the innocent flee, go into hiding, are killed or die (being unable to go about the business of staying alive). Nor would there be any less risk of total disaster in a large society, for it is not difficult to imagine the destruction or the immobilizing fear that one person, *unimpeded,* could cause in a city, say, the size of New York. There are, in other words, certain acts that one per-

---

*As far as earliest man is concerned, some paleoanthropologists, calling on the remarkable discoveries of recent years, hold just the opposite view to that of Hobbes, namely, that earliest man was extremely cooperative and nonaggressive, and that aggression was confined to the hunt and only in time did man turn it on himself. See *Lucy* by Donald C. Johanson and Maitland A. Edey (New York: Simon & Schuster, 1981), chapter 16, and *Origins,* by Richard E. Leakey and Roger Lewin (New York: Dutton, 1977), chapters 4, 8, 9.

son, *unimpeded*, can do that are truly enormous in their potential.

In short, given the desire to stay alive and to maintain a group*
we are logically compelled to do something—to remove the killer
(robber, etc.) from the group—to ostracize him; to cut off his
hands or feet; to segregate him (as in a jail); to kill him—not pri-
marily as a deterrent or an example to others, but because a group
cannot survive *one killer* (etc.) freely going about his business.

• But *which* killers, robbers, arsonists must be segregated or
otherwise punished—only those who are inclined to keep at it?
Only second offenders? Third offenders? Those who are insane?
Those who are doing it for kicks? Those who are doing it for
money? Those who don't have a "legitimate" excuse? Given the
desire to stay alive and to maintain a group as our guide, these may
appear, at first glance, difficult questions to answer for certainly a
group can survive one assault on one of its members, and even
another by the same person. However, since we have no way of
determining what the future plans of killers, arsonists, and muggers
really are (indeed, they may not know themselves); since we do
not know what would go on in the heads of some of the innocent
if everyone were allowed one PC violation; and since what is at
stake is the potential destruction of everything—therefore we have
no choice but to opt for the safest possible course, that is, to
punish first offenders. Looked at another way, there are acts that
we cannot allow one person to do or everyone to do once.

• The actual form of punishment for violators of the PC is not
compelled by our desire to live and to maintain a group, but is,
instead, a difficult judgment to make. Beyond the absolute necessity

---

*Actually "desire" should be plural, with one desire (to stay alive) leading,
logically, to the other (to maintain a group), but since the two are so interlinked
at this stage of my argument, I will continue to use the singular. There is, of
course, an interesting question as to which should come first (the group or the
individual), but since in either case we get the PC, this question can be postponed
for now. I shall refer to *a* group rather than *the* group, since I don't want to
preclude anyone from choosing to join a new group, or from radically altering the
political or social structure of the group he or she happens to be in.

of doing something to violators so that we can live, it is by no means easy to agree on what should be done to them, for while our shared desire demands action, *it is silent on specific forms of punishment.* Cutting off the hands of a thief may seem to many a cruel punishment, but it is not necessarily irrational, particularly in a society that cannot afford the time or the manpower to guard violators but doesn't wish to go so far as to dispatch them. Let me, at this point, acknowledge that certain people who violate the PC are no real threat to destroy everything if unchecked and that there are kinds of stealing, for example, that are not very serious. A six-year-old stealing a pencil from a classmate is not a clear and present danger to society. Nevertheless, such an act is wrong and demands some kind of punishment—if no more than condemnation—because the group must not idly stand by waiting only for dangerous manifestations of the act of stealing. What I am trying to get at here is that while there are degrees of stealing, they are all wrong and all demand some form of punishment.

• So far I have not said it is wrong for someone to kill (etc.), but only that it is wrong, incorrect, and incoherent *for us* to allow anyone to kill (etc.), given our desire to live and to maintain a group. The fundamental social contract—the initial handshake—is not a promise between us not to kill, assault, and rob one another, but rather to segregate or otherwise punish those who do.

However, once the PC is established, two consequences of great importance to the individual follow: (1) It is wrong, incorrect, and incoherent for us (i.e., the group) to punish or otherwise harm an innocent person, for this would breakdown the distinction between guilt and innocence and make the PC meaningless and, if carried far enough, would lead to the destruction of the group. This, in turn, leads to prototype definitions of injustice and unfairness, namely, it is unjust and unfair (and a threat of destruction to the group) to punish those who haven't done anything wrong. There is more to life than the PC and more to guilt than PC violations, but what I am trying to establish here is that there clearly are such things as injustice and unfairness. If a shared criterion says no to an act and I don't do it, it is unfair and unjust to punish me as if I had done it (e.g., a black being arrested for attempted rape because he whistled at a woman). (2) It is wrong, incorrect, and incoherent *for an individual* to kill or commit certain other acts if he or she desires to live (or at least to live as others live). In other words, once the PC has been established, a reality is created in which the killer, in killing risks his or her life (or the better part of it, depending on the actual punishment), and the basic question facing the would-be killer is: "Do I want to live or not?" If the answer is yes, then, *given reality*, it is wrong, incorrect, and incoherent of him or her to commit murder. As for whether murder, etc., is wrong in some other sense as well, I shall get to this question further on.

I may kill for passion or profit, but if my group (on which my life depends) permits killing, I am doomed, for my group is doomed. If killing is forbidden and I do it anyway, and am caught, I am also doomed. I am doomed in either case by compelling logic, a logic ultimately founded on the fact that *Homo sapiens*, standing naked, alone in the jungle or on the plain, have little chance of surviving. Thus the group; thus the PC. In those rare cases where an individual knows for sure that he can get away with murder, the act is still wrong—it's just that we can't catch him. Primary-code violations are a heavy burden for most of us, for what we sense, even if we don't understand it as such, is that certain acts threaten the destruction of everything—ourselves, our loved ones, the group; thus for most of us there is no getting away with them, and we must live with the terrible risk we have taken. The situation in which we *must* violate one of the PC proscriptions *in order* to keep alive—e.g., stealing food because there is no other course open to us—will be examined further on.

That many would-be killers (etc.) are under the guidance of a desire stronger than the desire to live is probably true, and the only hope is to try to spark their desire to live (perhaps by drawing attention to the terrible things we will do to them if they do kill) with the hope then that they will adjust their behavior accordingly. When there is no shared desire to appeal to, there is, in point of fact, not much to be said other than hollow rhetoric, but the rest of us—given our desire to live and to maintain a group—still know what we have to do.

• The list of acts that must be proscribed if the group is to survive (murder, robbery, arson, assault, pollution—the PC proscriptions) *is intended to be an exhaustive list.* I have in mind *only those acts* that if done freely by even *one person* would lead to the quick and certain demise of the group. (There are other acts that *if committed by a lot of people* would lead to the demise of the group— but this is a different matter, for discussion in the next chapter. It is also true that groups, themselves, can, as it were, institutionalize or sanction PC violations against some of their own subgroups. I will discuss this later on in a section titled "The Problem of Redheads"—technically speaking, a group could survive if it killed or enslaved all its redheads, and this raises an important question, but one that can only be answered after more of my argument has been developed.)

However, just as there are substantive and procedural aspects of law, so the PC has its procedural side: even in the most rudimentary group a number of other acts must be proscribed and violators punished, for they interfere *with the enforcement of the PC.* No member of the group may be allowed to bear false witness; no judge may accept a bribe; *every* violator must be punished; and the innocent must be left alone. While it is true that a society can tolerate considerable corruption of these procedural aspects of the PC (just as, in fact, a society can survive a considerable amount of violent crime) such corruption is still wrong, since it is a direct threat to the administration of the PC. Indeed, groups that allow too much corruption invariably end up in bloodshed as the PC simply breaks down, and there is either reform or the destruction of the group. The fact that even in the most corrupt society money is passed "under the table" is an indication that the participants know they are doing something wrong; doors are shut, voices drop, and words are replaced by gestures—even when the participants are those who actually run the country.

In summary: Given the generally shared desire to stay alive, and given the truth that (1) *Homo sapiens* have an obviously better chance of staying alive in a group than alone in the jungle or on the plain, and (2) there are certain acts that would destroy the group if one person were allowed to do them; it is, therefore, wrong, incorrect, and incoherent for the group to permit these acts. Furthermore, since these acts must be proscribed and violators must be punished, it is also wrong, incorrect, and incoherent of those who want to live (or at least to live as others live) to commit these acts. Putting the argument in its final elliptic form, "Murder (etc.) is wrong!"

I have not discussed behavior *between* groups and have barely touched on the treatment of certain subgroups *within* societies (Hitler and the Jews, Stalin and the peasants), but I will, and here, too, I will try to show that where there are unchecked PC violations, not only do death and destruction follow, but the destruction of everything becomes a real likelihood.

THE REAL WORLD

If I have been correct in my analysis, then there is a test that my theory must pass if it is to have any relevance to the real world: namely, either we must find that killers, arsonists, poisoners of the water supply, etc., are subject to punishment in every group—now and back to Pleistocene times—or we must find that a tribe or society without the PC is in the process of rapid deterioration. This is my argument: the PC is that without which there is nothing. The actual proof of my argument would be a considerable undertaking, but I don't believe it is necessary, for I think the mind of the reader has already done as much proving as is needed. Are you not pretty certain that if I dropped you anywhere on earth—even though you did not know the language, the customs, the laws, or the religion of the place I dropped you—that you would be in a lot of trouble if you killed, torched, robbed, or assaulted, and that, indeed, you would be breaking the rules of the society you were in?* While I have sent you on this trip, let me fortify the point

---

*If we were dropped in Lebanon or Northern Ireland in 1985 (and many other places at various times), we might be momentarily confused—and think that anything goes. But no, the faction that controlled the actual territory or neighborhood we were in would be daily (if crudely) administering the PC punishments *to its own members* who killed, robbed, or assaulted other members, and we, too, would be dealt with accordingly if we committed these PC violations. Furthermore, the fact that the PC didn't hold over the broad territories of Lebanon and Northern Ireland would be proof that when it doesn't hold, the group falls apart.

that the PC proscriptions are an exhaustive list: there are many other acts that you might be punished for (e.g., gambling, drinking alcohol, engaging in a homosexual act, having or performing an abortion) *but you wouldn't know ahead of time*, as you do with the PC acts, that you would be punished, and the only way to find out would be to make inquiries or observations. We can, I am arguing, be sure ahead of time only as far as the PC acts are concerned, and the reason is that if we didn't find them proscribed we wouldn't find human life.

Clearly, this method of testing my theory is less than scientific, and while my own random readings into the history of morality* have all supported my theory about the PC proscriptions, I must finally leave it to the reader or to others to do a more thorough job. Nevertheless, from my own readings I have a few caveats for those who would test the theory that groups have always had the PC proscriptions because they must have them to survive.

If you find an exception, make sure you see how the group turns out before you scrap the theory.† In my own readings my greatest despair and my greatest delight came from E. Adamson Hoebel's account of the Greenland Eskimos prior to their coming under the jurisdiction of Denmark.‡ Hoebel states that these Eskimos *allowed an initial killing* by a member of the tribe, and it was only repeated murder that became a "public crime punishable by death at the hands of an agent of the community." Since to allow even one killing is a clear violation of the PC, my theory

---

*Actually, there are very few books about the history of morality; what I really mean is my random readings in history, anthropology, and paleoanthropology looking for clues to the history of morality. Nor have I been ashamed to go to sources long discredited by serious students, for the pickings are slim enough without passing over men and women who, whatever the shortcomings of their theories and conclusions, accumulated a lot of facts that are generally not in dispute.

†At first glance Germany under Hitler might seem to be a monumental exception, but I will get to Hitler further on, and one of my points will be that Hitler and the Nazis *had* the PC (a Nazi who killed another Nazi was punished) but *they also violated* the PC. Even a group of murderers *must* have the PC, internally.

‡E. Adamson Hoebel, *The Law of Primitive Man* (New York: Atheneum, 1976), pp. 80-99; originally published by Harvard University Press, 1954.

would at best have to undergo a major overhaul. But wait—by the time we get to the end of the section on the Greenland Eskimos, we find that they might well have been heading toward extinction, had they not come under the rule of Denmark:

> But the weakness of the Eskimo system are [sic] evident. In a society in which manpower is desperately needed, in which occupational hazards destroy more men than society can afford, there is additional tragic waste in the killings which the *inchoate system permits*—indeed encourages. [Emphasis added.]

The system *was* incomplete, and consequently the Eskimos were in a lot of trouble because of the variation in the PC that they allowed. One may not always find such sweet revenge against those who do not have all the PC proscriptions, but my point is that not finding them is not enough to disprove the theory; one must know what happened to the group.

Another caveat: Do not be confused by the reasons given for the segregation of PC violators, or the absence of such familiar words as "law," "rules," "violator," "guilty," "innocent," "right," or "wrong"—*what matters is only the segregation!* According to Melvin Konner, who lived with the San (a nomadic tribe in the Kalahari Desert of Africa) for two years, "intractable violence . . . is so incomprehensible it seems to be classified more as a mental disorder than sin."* But however classified, those San who commit what I call the PC acts are usually killed if they don't flee first.† Indeed, if the hunter-gatherers of modern times are any indication of how Pleistocene man lived (and most anthropologists believe that they are probably much alike), then for eons of human existence PC violators may have been looked upon not as criminal but simply as dangerous to have around. James George Frazer writes about the attitude toward the treatment of "man-

---

*Melvin Konner, *The Tangled Wing* (New York: Holt, Rinehart & Winston, 1982), p. 7.

†Richard Borshay Lee, *The Kung San* (Cambridge: Cambridge University Press, 1979): see chapter 13, "Crime and Violence."

slayers" in a number of tribes, and the following passage about the Omahas of North America is typical:

> He had to observe certain stringent rules for a period which varied from two to four years. He must walk barefoot, and he might eat no warm food, nor raise his voice, nor look around. He was compelled to pull his robe about him and have it tied at the neck even in hot weather; he might not let it hang loose or fly open. He might not move his hands about, but had to keep them close to his body. He might not comb his hair, and it might not be blown about by the wind. When the tribe went out hunting, he was obliged to pitch his tent about a quarter of a mile from the rest of the people "lest the ghost of his victim should raise a high wind, which might cause damage." Only one of his kindred was allowed to remain with him at his tent. No one wished to eat with him. . . . At the end of his long isolation the kinsmen of the murdered man heard his crying and said, "It is enough. Begone, and walk among the crowd. Put on moccasins and wear a good robe."*

This is punishment indeed, but it is not meant as punishment. The requirements on clothing, hair, and raising one's voice are all meant to keep the manslayer as inconspicuous as possible from the ghost of his victim. He is kept from the body of the group and never has more than one person with him so that if he is noticed, the innocent won't be harmed by the "high wind" the ghost may cause. The rationale is murky, to say the least; nevertheless, *the ultimate reason* the Omahas would give for this treatment of the manslayer would be in harmony with the logic of my argument— the protection of life and the group.

One other point: The strong emotions of hatred and vengeance that we usually associate with PC violations are apparently lacking among the Omahas, since it is the kin of the victim who invite the manslayer back to the tribe. This was apparently the case, too, with the Greenland Eskimos, for certainly any group that can allow an initial killing cannot be said to be guided by the emotions of hatred and vengeance.

---

*James George Frazer, *The Golden Bough* (New York: Macmillan, 1922), p. 251.

Frazer's story may be nothing more than a story, but stories like it have been told by many others, and Frazer's conclusion, that the taboos and segregations were founded on the desire to live (or the fear of death, if you will) and the survival of the group, I have not found disputed.

THE PRECISE DEFINITION OF MORALITY

Up to now I have not used the word "morality," and the question arises as to whether the PC is morality or any part of it. But before turning to this question let me make some preliminary observations.

In the midst of all the heated debate over what is right and wrong, if we listen carefully, we find remarkable agreement on the precise meaning of the word "morality." Morality is an ultimate guide to action. It is universal, timeless, not subject to compromise, truth (not opinion), it demands the punishment of the immoral,* and, finally, morality does not guide on every decision facing us.

If a question is moral, or is perceived to be moral, then we cannot compromise our position, since we compromise in the name of something more important to us, and there is nothing more important than morality—and indeed, if we did compromise we would be immoral, for we would be sacrificing morality to some less important consideration. (I mean by compromise not just reaching a middle ground—clearly impossible on such questions as abortion and capital punishment—but giving in to the other side, or accepting defeat.) Morality is universal and timeless, because if it were not, we would need a higher-order criterion for judging the "morality" of our time and place, and our "morality" would not be an ultimate guide. It would not, therefore, be morality, but

---

*On this point—punishment—there is, at least in today's world, some disagreement. For example, some people may hold homosexual acts to be immoral but not want them punished. I will argue in the next chapter that people who say this are confused; what they really mean is that homosexuality is not immoral, for a live-and-let-live attitude toward anything truly immoral is the end of morality and is total relativism.

rather "just our way of doing things," and we would be faced with the question "How do we know our way of doing things is the right way?"

Morality is truth; for if it were not truth it would be opinion, and the door would be open to relativism and anarchy. Morality allows for some "free choices"; for if it did not we would be overwhelmed with proscriptions and could hardly think or act, given this extra consideration to our every thought and act. Finally, we must punish the immoral; for otherwise the guide would be meaningless, since everyone could do what he or she wanted, and this would lead to the destruction of everything, since it would allow killers to do what they wanted.

My point is that when we enter the whirlwind of what passes for moral discourse, we discover, by listening to common usage of the word "morality," *a precise definition* of the term—with people saying all the time, in perfectly logical sequence, "It's a moral question, it's not a matter of opinion, there is no room for compromise, and the truth is . . . ." And when a word has a precise defintion, the Basic Rule applies, which is to say we can't do as we like with it without causing confusion. The only problem now is whether such an ultimate guide actually exists or whether everyone is asserting nothing more than personal illusion and calling it morality.

IS THERE SUCH A THING AS MORALITY?

The PC proscriptions are found everywhere but is this guide an ultimate guide? Or, in other words, do we have morality: an ultimate and universal guide to action? When it comes to morality we cannot say, "This act is immoral, but even more important . . ." for there is nothing more important than morality. Therefore, at first glance it would appear that the PC proscriptions *are not* founded on an ultimate guide, because *we can say*, "I want to live, but even more important, I want to save my child who is in that burning building." And more than one ardent nationalist has said, "I will gladly die and send my children to die for the fatherland." Soldiers, police, and fire personnel risk their lives for the sake of others. Daredevils risk their lives for fame and glory. Radicals risk their lives to change the political structure of the group. While, for most of us, the desire to stay alive is our ultimate consideration in most situations, we can imagine situations where it might not be, given a choice that involved other people.

But wait—remove the desire to stay alive from my model and substitute one of these other desires that on rare occasions do come up, and observe: The model still stands, everything remains the same, since if I choose to die for the fatherland, or for a revolutionary social order, or so that my child may live, it is absolutely essential that I establish the PC, if it has not already been established, before I die. For without the PC there is nothing, and I will have suffered the worst fate possible—I will have died for nothing; the mayhem that follows if the PC is not in place will soon destroy my child, and the fatherland, and the new social order.

On a less heroic level—everything still remains the same. If one's passion is to play chess, one must first establish the PC, if it hasn't already been established. Tennis? Business? Art? Computers? Literature? Philosophy?—one must first establish the PC. Let one killer, one arsonist, one poisoner of the water supply, etc., do what he or she wants, and everything comes to an end. And now, at last, the true desire on which the PC is actually founded begins to emerge; a desire that is deep in most of us but that, at least until the nuclear age, most people were not conscious of. Most of us don't want everything destroyed.*

---

*But there is something peculiar here, and very frightening. I mention this desire to people and they, now suddenly sitting on top of the world (and able to blow it up) because of the example I have set up, wave their hands like Nero and say, "I don't care if everything is destroyed or not—I really don't." Yet take a dime from them, make love to their wives or husbands, cheat them at poker and they go crazy—yet these are all things that, obviously, would disappear if everything disappeared. But my worry is that there is truth here too (in what people say when you put them in charge of everything); I believe that the destructive and self-destructive urge increases in some people the more powerful they become, and that we who want life to go on must be more cautious in whom we allow to come to power, and we would be if we better understood the nonsense some leaders talk and what they call morality. More on this point in a moment. See also

So there are acts that, if permitted, would lead to to the destruction of everything, and nobody, or practically nobody, wants that. This desire is the ultimate and all-but-universal guide in situations where the destruction of everything is possible, since it would sound nonsensical to argue, "This act, if permitted, would lead to the destruction of everything, but even more important. . . ." Which is to say that an ultimate and all-but-universal guide does exist, which is further to say that morality exists! Mankind has always had enough strong rhetoric against murder (etc.)—"contrary to the word of God," "a crime against nature," "violation of basic human rights"—to have been able to survive, up to now, without understanding the true nature of morality (the real desire on which it is founded). But still, as I will try to show, mankind's confusion about morality has been terribly costly in terms of human life and suffering.

Now we can begin to appreciate the nature of all the confusion about morality. Morality is one of those peculiar words having a precise if hidden definition—it is an ultimate and universal guide to action and is, in fact, *the desire that everything not be destroyed.* Morality not only exists but countless times it actually guides us as we lock up murderers, arsonists, robbers,* and those who assault, because we deem them to have violated our desire that everything not be destroyed. Thus it is that the word "morality," having a precise if hidden definition, falls under the Basic Rule, which means that we cannot do with the word as we like and that *we are locked in* and can only use the word according to its precise de-

---

Iceman Comics, June 1985, where the "force" that calls itself Oblivion (and is opposed by Iceman) is in a position to destroy the world and decides to do it because it is, as he says, "the only way to find peace."

*Returning to the Jones hybrid for a moment: Embezzlement is a form of robbery, and it is immoral—let one man or woman freely enter the banks that exist in most societies and do what he or she wants, and farmers, truckers, and merchants might not be paid; and if the embezzler struck again every time we tried to restructure the economic system, the disaster would be incalculable. Jones was immoral, but he paid his debts to society and his immorality did not figure in our calculations. As to the question of whether we are morally obliged to hire him, there is no moral answer to that question—it is a matter of opinion, as we shall see in the next chapter.

finition, unless we give a linguistic clue to some special or metaphorical usage, or unless our intention is to deceive, confuse, or infuriate. To say "That act is morally wrong," and to mean anything other than it would be incorrect and incoherent of us to allow this act, given our shared desire that everything not be destroyed is to be in violation of the Basic Rule; is to be guilty of the unannounced metaphor; and is to repeat and encourage the kind of thinking that, as we shall see, has been nothing less than horrendous in its consequences to mankind. But before looking for trouble let me finish up with the PC for there is an important question that has to be answered, namely, whether or not I (we, mankind) have committed the naturalistic fallacy.

THE BASIC WORDS

Let us look for a moment at the meaning of the basic words ("right," "wrong," "good," and "bad") in light of my argument to this point, for the word "good," in particular, was the key word in Moore's relentless questioning of the theologians and the naturalists: How do you know the voice you heard was necessarily that of a good being? How do you know that pleasure is necessarily a good thing? And this kind of questioning apparently leads to an infinite regression, for the question will be raised of any *thing* (natural or supernatural) that is proposed as an ultimate guide to action.

We have already noted that the words "right," "wrong," "good," "bad" have another set of precise definitions in situations where a decision is not necessarily called for. They can mean an act in keeping with (or not in keeping with) a shared desire or criterion. Thus we say that Medea did something wrong in killing her children, even though no action is called for on our part. Now let me concentrate on this other set of precise definitions, for it is here that we find tremendous confusion in the area of morality, confusion that Moore recognized in part but only in part, and consequently he fell into an even deeper morass.

The confusion was originally started by theologians when they gave a "profound" definition to the word "good," namely, God is good. (And I say "profound" because God is a profound concept.) Then, as God began to fade from the design, philosophers jumped to the (erroneous) conclusion that what was desperately needed was a new definition of the word "good," and they came up with many of them—good is pleasure, good is happiness, good is what is natural. No! Good is a humble, hardworking word with a precise definition: it means an act in keeping with a criterion—*any criterion*. (The devil's assistant: "People are following in your path more than ever before." The devil: "Good!") Good never needed a definition; it had a precise (if hidden) definition, and it couldn't be given a new definition without confusing everything—which in fact happened, because everyone kept slapping new definitions on it. The real struggle in moral philosophy is not with the meaning of the word "good" but to find an ultimate and all-but-universal guide to action, and one can probe the meaning of the word "good" ("What is morally good?") from here to eternity and never even face the real question at hand. What is morally good is answered in a phrase: an act in keeping with an ultimate and all-but-universal guide to action.

But unfortunately the struggle centered around the meaning of the word "good" and it was into this linguistic mess that Moore entered, and asked his question. To the utilitarians: "How do you know that pleasure, itself, is necessarily a good thing?" His question seemed to make sense, but he didn't understand why it made sense, and thus he was led to the most absurd conclusion of all, namely, that the word "good" is indefinable*—a conclusion that few philosophers could accept and that eventually caused Moore to acknowledge that he didn't know what he was talking about.†

The reason Moore's question to the utilitarians seems to make sense is not that "good" is indefinable, but that it has a precise

---

*Good, Moore argued, is like the color yellow: we know it when we see it, but we can't define it. See *Principia Ethica* (Cambridge, England: Cambridge University Press, 1903), pp. 7-8.

†"All my supposed proofs were certainly fallacious. . . . And I think perhaps it [good] is definable: I do not know. But I also think that very likely it is indefinable." "Is Goodness a Quality?" *Philosophical Papers* (London: Allen and Unwin, 1959), p. 98.

definiton, and Moore is bringing this definition to mind (sub-liminally at least) when he asks his question. Good means some-thing in keeping with a criterion (good in terms of what?), and so Moore's question "How do you know that pleasure is good?" really means "By what criterion have you choosen your criterion?" and this seems to be a legitimate question, and it became all the more legitimate as people began to lose faith in a talking God and scores of new criteria were proposed as the foundation for the traditional list of "dos and don'ts." Furthermore, it has seemed to many people who have thought about Moore's metaethical ques-tion that it can be asked indefinitely of any *thing* natural or super-natural and that both the naturalists and the theologians are guilty of a fallacy. I bring up all this history because Moore's question must now be faced, which cannot be done unless we understand what I believe to be its true meaning—by what criterion have you chosen your criterion?

THE NATURALISTIC FALLACY

Have I (we, mankind) committed the naturalistic fallacy? Moore was precise. He said he meant to include under the heading "na-ture" "any mental attitude whatever—either of feeling, or of de-siring."* This, of course, would include the desire that everything not be destroyed. Supposedly, Moore would now ask: "How do you know that this desire is, itself, a good thing?" which, as I have just tried to show, really means "By what criterion have you chosen this desire as your ultimate criterion?"

My answer to Moore is no—I, we, mankind, have committed no error, since literally there is *nothing* beyond the desire that everything not be destroyed: no talk, no criterion, no desire, no philosophy, nothing. If we don't have this desire and live according to its demands, we have nothing. Which is to say, among other things, that we are not involved in an infinite regression. The desire that everything not be destroyed is the end of the line—it is impossible to make sense when saying, "This act will lead to the

---

Ethics (London: Oxford University Press, 1912), p. 138.

destruction of everything, but even more important. . . ." The very reason Moore's question makes sense when asked of the various spurious criteria is that, subliminally at least, the mind recognizes that pleasure and the other proposed criteria are not ultimate guides and therefore resists calling them so, or at least causes us to doubt that they are ultimate guides. The reason Moore's question does not work when asked of the true guide is that there is, literally, nothing beyond it.

A man with his finger on a button that can blow up the world may ponder whether to do it, but ultimately either he desires that life go on or he doesn't, and if he doesn't, there is no rational way to reach him—no higher-order desire or criterion to appeal to. This means that we have morality (the desire that everything not be destroyed as our ultimate guide) or we have nothing, which is exactly our true situation. I can only wonder if Moore, had he been asked, would still think his question to be of any significance (asking, in effect, that we justify the desire that life go on by some higher-order desire or criterion) or if he would not just say, "Yes, this guide is morality; it's what we were looking for, and it is, indeed, that beyond which (and without which) there is nothing." But far be it for me to put words in Moore's mouth or to restrict philosophers in anything they wish to consider—just as long as they join with me first in establishing the PC (for without it we cannot discuss anything).

Am I not claiming what everyone else has claimed, namely, that my view of morality is the right one and everyone else's is wrong? Yes, definitely *but everything I have said is verifiable.* When we go to common usage, do we or do we not find a precise definition of the word "morality"? Is it not true that if a word has a precise definition then we are locked in and cannot do as we wish with the word? Is it not true that the desire that everything not be destroyed is an ultimate and all-but-universal guide, i.e., it meets the precise definition of morality? Does this desire, in fact, guide with respect to certain acts, and are these acts proscribed everywhere through all time? Are the PC proscriptions true? (Or should we really say, "In *my opinion* murder is wrong?") And when you answer all these questions—and I believe I have done this—do you or do you not come up with morality?—a real thing in the real world. I may be proved wrong, but since I have proved all these propositions (at least to my own satisfaction), I will do the only thing I can do, and that is to continue with my argument—with the problem of why, if morality actually exists and exists everywhere, there is so much mayhem in the world.

THE MYSTIFICATION OF MORALITY

"We are apt to be haunted by the thought of a lawgiver when it is a question of what we are to do, and the thought that somehow and somewhere it is written down is very compelling indeed."* Such is the mystification of morality—and I mean by mystification (following Professor Foot's lead) the displacement of desire by something more elegant: self-evident truth, natural law, basic rights, God; something above and beyond man, out there somewhere; something that is so offended by certain acts that such acts are seen not as a threat to man but as an affront to the eternal; something such that we do not see ourselves as petty scriveners scratching out our rules and regulations in the earnest desire to save our own skins, but as soliders in service to the transcendent—such is the mystification of morality that to think of wrong as meaning "incorrect given a shared desire" may seem trifling. Yet to think of wrong in any other sense when it comes ot the PC acts is superfluous at best and dangerous at worst—leading to confusion where we dare not be confused. What other sense do we dare think of beyond the potential destruction of everything?

Even if we retrict ourselves to talking cold truth to killers, what we can say, though it won't be grand or emotionally satisfying to us, is no mean matter, at least to them. We can say, "Leaving aside our hatred and disgust at what you have done; leaving aside our deepest intuition that what you have done is wrong; leaving aside the laws of nature; and leaving aside the word of God (on cold-blooded killing) as spoken to all people in all times—we dare not let you get away with it."

---

*Philippa Foot, "Morality and Art," in *Philosophy As It Is*, ed., Ted Honderich and Miles Burnyeat. (New York: Penguin, 1979), p. 17.

The churches may crumble, the prophets of God may prove to be frauds, the laws of nature may be relative, and we may not be able to reach our deepest intuitions, but still we must put away killers, and this truth, to me, is satisfying: a certainty in a shaky and uncertain world. Only if we don't want to live will this truth seem uncertain, but even then there will be *certainty*—we shall die.

Societies have become so large and complex, and the threat from beasts in the jungle so remote for most of us, and morality so mystified, that we tend to lose sight of the connection between life, the group, and the rules against certan acts. (I have spoken with those who say, "Well, you're just talking about the criminal code," as if that were minor business compared to the truly serious business of morality.) But drop the rules and punishments against these acts and we will observe, quickly enough, a society falling apart, and in the process our lives and the lives of our loved ones will be in grave danger—now more than ever, since there is no place to flee. In such chaos it might not sound too odd were someone to say—despairing of the endless debates over the true nature of morality and the meaning of its terms—that dropping these rules was a mistake, incorrect, incoherent. And, where these rules exist—and, in fact, they exist everywhere—even the killer sitting on death row and having mocked morality all his life might wonder, on occasion, if he, too, hadn't made a mistake.

MORAL MONSTERS

When we say "wrong," the question "Wrong in terms of what shared desire?" may seem deeply disturbing if we are faced with a monster who cares nothing for the primary code. It might be argued that I am letting monsters off the hook—indeed, giving them a certain philosophical legitimacy, since what the monster is doing (e.g., throwing babies in the lake) is right in terms of its background desire (to rid the world of babies) and wrong *only* if viewed in light of *our* desire to live and maintain a group. This concern (that I am letting monsters off the hook) arises from the *illusion* that there is a transcendent authority to appeal to in the first place that, independent of us, condemns moral monsters. But none of this matters—for even if there were a transcendent logic, it would either tell us to get monsters out of the way, in which case it would be redundant, or it would be wrong—given our desire to live.

I do not see any reason that we can't adjust to our true situation, just as we got over the traumatic discovery that the earth is not the center of the universe. Life is still wonderfully mysterious, and the ancient question "Why is there something rather than nothing?" is still as fascinating as ever, even if the earth is not the center of the universe and the PC truths come from a generally shared desire.

GUILT AND CONSCIENCE

Another concern about my argument, I know from discussing it with others, is that it appears to give children and would-be violators too much choice (if you don't want to live, you can do whatever you want) and doesn't require the conscience and guilt of traditional morality. But the truth is that those in our midst who don't care about their own lives have always been a menace to the rest of us, and they will reject whatever criterion we may offer or twist it in support of their own behavior. If we faced these self-destructive types for what they are, we might better reject the nonsense they often talk, and not get involved with them, or their apologists, on the dangerous level to which they often try to drag us (where the basic words become unanchored and we are easily disoriented)—and to which we too often allow ourselves to be dragged, uncertain as we are of the true nature of right and wrong.*

As for children, it seems to me that we can safely substitute self-interest for mystery without adding to the number of murderers and arsonists in our midst. We can say, "Do you want to live?" "Yes." "Then don't do that!" This would seem to me to have a powerfully healthful effect on the young mind. The child's

---

*See Jack Abbott, In the Belly of the Beast (New York: Random House, 1981), and Norman Mailer's perfervid apologia for Abbott at the latter's trial for the killing of Richard Adan. The more extensive coverage of Mailer's remarks was in the New York Post (January 18-24, 1982), but see also, the New York Times for the same dates.

guilt will not arise from having offended the transcendent or mysterious, but in having risked the loss of everything—true guilt, if you will.*

Furthermore, most of the killing and torching and bombing in the world is done not by street criminals but by those in service to what I shall call their secondary-code morality. Since there is great confusion surrounding the nature of right and wrong, there is great confusion as to why we are killing, burning, and bombing one another—and I think this is, in point of fact, a true statement. If we faced morality for what it is, there might be less death and destruction, not more. But I am running ahead of myself, for there can be no support for these broad statements until we understand the other half of what passes for morality—the dark side that gets us hating, fearing, and killing strangers.

MORAL OBLIGATION

Morality entails obligation. But since the nature of morality is not understood for what it is, the nature of moral obligation has not been understood either. In particular, the group has always tried to lay an obligation on the individual to act this way and not that way, and in time this obligtion has been understood to come from something even higher than the group, e.g., God saying, "Thou shalt not kill." This has all been very risky, for it totally confuses the nature of moral obligation. Thus when five-year-olds or would-be killers ask "Why ought I to be moral?" we may well, as we have

---

*At some other time I would like to explore the following hypothesis: Guilt ultimately stems from fear of death—it is a bad feeling that comes over us when, by our acts, we fear we have offended something (God, society, parents) that will, therefore, abandon us—to burn in hell, or be thrown in the streets, or rot in jail. If we do something that might cause this but are not caught, we still have this dreadful worry. For certainly with guilt there is belief that we have offended something or someone, and we care because we fear rejection and abandonment—which for the young child would mean death. Finally, I would argue that today's struggle against guilt is often a struggle against the bad feeling we get when we have done nothing really wrong except in the eyes of an authority which itself needs serious questioning.

so often done in the past, stumble for an answer; and if we can't find one on which even nonviolators can agree, our own sense of obligation may be replaced by a troubling sense of relativism. The obligation of morality is *on us* to put killers (etc.) away, and what killers (etc.) think or what obligation they accept or don't accept is irrelevant to morality. Now, I am sure there are those who will argue that as a practical matter it is wise to try to lay an obligation on five-year-olds (that it has a vital deterrent factor), but my own view is that it is far safer to explain to them the facts of moral life. When it comes to morality, any confusion is a very risky business and we dare not be confused or pass on confusion for any reason, however well intended.

THE HAUNTING QUESTION

Still a haunting question remains: Can't something be wrong even though it is not wrong given a shared desire or a verifiable proposition?* Can't one person be right and the rest of the world wrong? Yes, but when the voice in the wilderness is right and everyone else is wrong, what it is right about is *that what people are doing will lead to the frustration of a generally shared desire.* If, at present or in the future, what we are doing (or sanctioning) will not frustrate a generally shared desire, then the act is not wrong, for frustrating a generally shared desire is entailed in the very concept of wrong when the word is being used according to its precise definition in decision-making situations. Any other use of the word probably means that there is no shared desire or verifiable proposition relevant to a shared desire—and is probably no more than one person or one group telling another person or group, "What I want, what we want, I believe you and your group should want too, and here,

---

*Keep in mind that there are two truths in a hybrid. One is the *truth* of the hybrid statement itself, namely, that this decision holds the best chance of satisfying the shared desire. The other is the *verifiable proposition* (e.g., embezzlers are a thousand times greater risk to embezzle than nonembezzlers) that is found in the background argument. Thus when I use the phrase "not wrong given a shared desire *or* verifiable proposition," I am talking about the background argument and I mean that one or maybe both of the essential elements are missing.

in my opinion, is why," The least confusing way to say this is to say it, and leave right and wrong out of it. Having basic desires in conflict is trouble enough without making things worse by accusing the other side, in effect, of being blind, crazy, or demonic, as it would be if it were truly rejecting the logical consequences of a generally shared desire and verifiable proposition (e.g., if the other side was arguing that there is nothing wrong with arson). But by definition, haunting questions won't go away, and I will return to this one as we go along.

RIGHT AND GOOD

Given the desire to live and to maintain a group, certain acts are right, good, correct, and coherent of us to perform—crying wolf when a wolf is coming, putting one's finger in a leaking dike, finding those who are lost, helping those who have met with disaster, etc.,—and it is to the individual's advantage and the group's advantage to praise, celebrate, and otherwise encourage these acts. (The question of how much an individual is obliged to risk for the sake of the group is, however, *a difficult matter of opinion*, since the degree of obligation in this case is not logically compelled by the desire to stay alive—a point I will elaborate on in the next chapter.) It is also right (good, correct, coherent) *of us* not to allow any member of the group to reach a position in which *the only way* he or she can live (i.e., have the things necessary to stay alive) is by violating the PC, e.g., by stealing. This is a delicate point in practice, but sound in theory. Morality simply breaks down when an individual finds his or her life threatened *by adhering to it* (e.g., by not stealing I will die) and it is essential that the group not allow this to happen if it can possibly help it.

While it is right, good, correct, and coherent of us to commit and encourage certain acts, I will, for the most part, concentrate on the wrong and the bad of morality, because right and good acts don't fall into neat categories as do those acts that must be proscribed. But if we get a firm grip on what is wrong, we will have a better chance of understanding what is right, and—more important—what is *neither right nor wrong*.

MANKIND'S INCREASING CONFUSION ABOUT THE NATURE OF MORALITY

My search has been for the logic of morality and not its historical origins, and my argument is that however confused man has been about the nature of morality, the logic of the PC proscriptions has, somehow, almost always forced itself on him, and he has always gotten a jolt of truth for the PC hybrids. Nevertheless, when we get to the secondary codes in the next chapter, history will be more important to my argument and I think I will be able to show that with *the passage of time* mankind has become *increasingly confused* about the nature of morality, and this confusion has led to increasingly horrible consequences. By way of introducing the next chapter, let me call on my random readings in the history of morality and point out two related phenomena: mankind's increasing confusion and the barbarity of immoral leaders who rise to power by manipulating the language of morality and play on the people's confusion.

Pleistocene man (if today's hunter-gatherers are any indication of how he lived and what he believed) segregated and tabooed the "manslayer" for the safety of the group and the preservation of life, and he (Pleistocene man) would probably have told you as much if you had asked him. His penultimate reason for segregating the manslayer was murky (fear of ghosts raising storms against the manslayer), but his ultimate reason was right according to the logic of the PC: the manslayer was segregated because he was a danger to the group given the power of the forces out to get him.

When we get to the earliest Egyptians things begin to get more confused. It is then that we discover what may be the first moral locutions (first reference, 4000 B.C.), namely, "he who does what is hated," for the guilty, and "he who does what is loved," for the innocent.* Already the Egyptians have made a major error—*the emotional reaction* to murder (etc.) is not important to the PC proscriptions, and as we saw with the San, the Omahas, and the Greenland Eskimos, there is no indication that killing has always

---

*James Henry Breasted, *The Dawn of Conscience* (New York: Scribner's, 1933), p. 142.

been hated. But still, if all the Egyptians did hate killing, robbery, arson, etc., it could be argued that strong emotion (instead of fear of the ghosts of murder victims) was doing a constructive job, since it was leading to the PC proscriptions, at least in the minds of those talking about morality. And if one were to ask an early Egyptian, "Why are they hanging that man?" the answer, "Because he did what is hated," would explain something. But the door would be open to the question "Why do you punish those you hate?" and unless this question was answered properly (separating punishment from hate, and recognizing that hatred merely accompanies the PC logic), we would slip into deeper confusion. Which we (mankind) did, as we wrestled with the error of the initial moral locutions.

At about this same time (4000 B.C.) the Egyptian word for "correct" (as in a correct answer, or correct time) was *maat*—a simple, cognitive, hard-working word. But by the year 3200 B.C. this honest word had become *Maat*, meaning "right" or "righteous," and it took the place of "he who does what is loved." And now if one were to ask an Egyptian, "Why are they hanging that man?" he would reply, "Because he didn't do what is *Maat*." And asked to explain what in the world he was talking about and why the man was *really* being hanged, the Egyptian, in all probability, could not have explained anything.

But at least God wasn't in the moral design at this time. In Egypt, and other societies as well, He was (mercifully) still centuries away. But in time He was put in the picture, and thereafter when one asked why they were hanging that man, the answer was because he violated a commandment of God, which is almost as far from the logic of the PC as it is possible to get. Finally, we get to Moore, who said that "good" is indefinable, and everyone threw up his or her hands and stopped asking questions.

None of this would matter—since the PC has somehow always remained in place despite our growing confusion—were it not for the fact that so much else passes under the heading of morality, and that political leaders have always misused the language of morality to rise to power, and that some political leaders are immoral, and that the weapons at hand are ever greater.

When it comes to the question of whether or not to allow one cold-blooded killer to wander about the streets killing people, groups have generally known what to do, despite their confusion about the nature of morality and despite the fact that the killer may have some "moral" rhetoric to account for his killing (e.g., "doing God's will"). But let the killer attract a few followers with his rhetoric and the rest of the world may become confused and dangerously immobilized. While the reason for our confusion about bands of killers cannot be fully understood until we examine the nature of secondary codes, part of the reason can be explained now.

Once two or more killers come together, a new group has been formed in the world (even though this group may share the same territory as another group), and the first thing it must establish *internally*, if it is to survive and succeed at the business of killing, is the PC. Once the PC is established, this killer group will be carrying out justice with respect to its own members, and there will be accounts of its "womenfolk" hugging babies and the killers hugging both. Too, there will be a "charismatic leader" who will use the language of morality to explain the killing (e.g., "to make it a better world") and to carry the killing as far as he or she can take it, for the leader of killers must be a quintessential killer with no other thoughts in mind, beyond the rhetoric needed to support the killing. Invariably he or she will gather extraordinary powers. And invariably, too, the killing will progress until the world wakes up or the leader dies.

The point I am trying to make is that if a leader is willing to kill the innocent to make it a better world, the safest course for *everyone* is to look upon him as a killer and not as an idealist, for the truth is, I believe, that he or she is far more turned on by the battle than the end, and will keep the battle (and killing) going on right down to wiping out half the palace guard, and then half of what remains, and so on. Or, in other words, it is the killing and not the rhetoric that accompanies the battle that is important and would be understood as important if we were not so confused about the nature of right and wrong.

In retrospect mankind has generally sensed the mental imbalance and the extreme threat posed by such leaders as Alexander the Great, Attila the Hun, Genghis Khan, Napoleon, Hitler, Stalin, and Mao Tse-tung,* but at the time these leaders lived it was often difficult to articulate the threat because of the confusion about right and wrong; each leader's successful manipulation of these basic words; and the leader's claim that he didn't want to destroy everything, but only make it a better world for the living. In today's world the threat of such leaders (e.g., Muammar Qaddafi and Ayatollah Khomeini) is seen somewhat more acutely, for the idea of such a leader idly pushing the nuclear button (if it is in his control) is recognized as quite real.

Hitler wasn't immoral because he killed six million Jews, he was immoral because he killed one Jew; when he killed one Jew, there was a risk that he might kill more; when he killed all the Jews, there was a risk that he might go on to kill other groups; when he killed other groups, there was a risk that he would blow up the world for the same reason he killed his first victim (whatever reason that really was), which is to say that Hitler was the quintessential example of the point I have been trying to make—allow a killer of one person to go freely about his or her business and we are doomed. Hitler was finally stopped, but he never would have begun if he had not been a master of manipulating the language of morality to his ends, and if people had not been so susceptible to such manipulation because of their failure to understand the nature of morality—which brings us to the secondary codes.

---

*Unleashing the Cultural Revolution was Mao's last attempt to keep the killing going, but he was too old.

Chapter Three

The Secondary Codes

"Gambling is wrong," "Abortion is wrong," and "Capital punishment is wrong" are all false hybrids (as they would be if we changed "wrong" to "right" or "a right"); they are unannounced metaphors and are statements in violation of the Basic Rule—or so I will try to show. So, too, are statements concerning alcohol, homosexual acts, vivisection, euthanasia, interracial marriage, premarital sex, prostitution, number of wives, divorce, freedom of speech, freedom of expression, pornography, drugs, etc., when put in the objective hybrid form. These acts are substantively different from the PC acts in that they would not cause the destruction of the group if we allowed one person to do them freely or everyone to do them once. Looked at another way, when we turn to the guide that gives us the PC proscriptions, it fails to give us clear direction on these other acts (e.g., we ask: Given the desire that everything not be destroyed, what should our position be on gambling? but we don't get a clear answer). Now if we allow one person to do any one of these acts then we must (logically) allow everyone to do them, for otherwise we would have an arbitrary system of punishment that might threaten the administration of the PC itself. Let law enforcement people punish who they want and soon there won't be any law, morality, or anything else. But this (allowing one person to do the act) raises the possibility of *enormous numbers of* people doing the act— which, in turn, raises the specter of total disaster. I will get to this problem later on for it is key to our understanding of what passes for morality, but for now the important point is that there is a sharp distinction between the PC acts and all other acts in that we cannot allow *one person* to do the former, but we can allow one person to do the latter without creating an immediate threat to everything. Looked at another way, morality (the ultimate guide, the desire that everything not be destroyed) is clearly at stake in one case, but not in the other.

Nevertheless, these acts (drinking, gambling, abortion, etc.) have been called into serious question by various groups at various times, and have been called morally wrong in one place but not in another. (They *are*, of course, serious questions because how we decide them sets the *very quality of life* for a group, but what I will be arguing is that they are not *moral questions!*) The acts that a group proscribes *because* they are held to be morally wrong even though they are not in violation of the PC guide, I will refer to as a group's secondary code.

All groups have the PC proscriptions. However, no two groups have the same list of secondary-code proscriptions. But since no distinction is generally recognized between the two codes, a group's Code (capitalized to indicate both codes) is morality, as far as it is concerned.

Many other matters besides the ones I have just mentioned are, or have been, perceived by some individuals and groups as moral, including forms of government and economic systems, as in "Communism is evil" and "Capitalism is basically immoral." And some formerly burning secondary-code questions such as divorce, alcohol, and gambling have—in the United States, for example— become "free choices" within certain legislative guidelines.

The fact that secondary-code acts are substantively different from PC acts does not, automatically, mean that they are not subject to a moral guide. We can have, theoretically, two or more ultimate and all-but-universal guides, just as long as the acts they cover never put them in conflict (so that an act will satisfy one guide but frustrate the other). However, on the face of it, the broad disagreement over whether to proscribe secondary-code acts (which is not true of the PC acts) and the fact that some people don't consider some of these questions to be moral at all would seem to be clear evidence that they are not subject to a universal guide. Thus I say, for example, that "Gambling is wrong" is a false hybrid, since it looks identical in form to "Murder is wrong" but it doesn't have a hybrid argument behind it.

Now a haunting question arises: Couldn't half the world be wrong? Yes and no. No, because the concept of wrong entails a shared desire or criterion. Yes, because half the world could be blind to a desire or criterion that it does, in fact, hold but that it has allowed other and lesser considerations to get in the way of. But now that we have the PC guide in hand, I can see no evidence that any ultimate guide other than the PC guide exists or that half the world is blind, for if such a guide did exist, it would—after eons of human existence—have guided almost all of us to the same conclusion *on at least one of these acts,* and in fact there is no general agreement on any of them. But the haunting question persists— how do I know that I have defined the word "morality" correctly, or that common usage (an ultimate and all-but-universal guide) should be the standard of its definition, or that common misusage (people calling anything important to them morality) is not also correct? The answer is—and to repeat—that we are *locked in,* assuming our intention is not to deceive, confuse, or infuriate. Morality is one of those peculiar words to which common usage has given a precise, if hidden, definition and it is used successfully countless times each day according to its precise definition—e.g., murders (etc.) *are* immoral. And any other use of a word with a precise definition without giving a linguistic clue to its special usage (saying, for example, "In *my opinion* abortion is wrong—or a right") is a violation of the Basic Rule, which must lead to confusion and anger. Which is exactly what we find when we go to the real world, and for this very reason, i.e., the constant misuse of the word "morality." Our situation is similar to any situation where we have given something a name. If we have decided to call the red, round, and tasty thing an apple, then it is nonsensical to ask, "How do we *know* what we are calling an apple is *really* an apple?" This holds for the word "morality" as well. It means an ultimate guide to action; furthermore, such a guide truly exists, and so if an act doesn't threaten morality, then it is not a matter of morality. Thus, I say that gambling, abortion, homosexuality, etc., are not moral questions.

(To scream that *this act* really is a matter of morality—when it is not—is only to express one's psychological state, not unlike when Bill screamed "Boozer *is* the wrong man for the job" when, in fact, Boozer is neither the right man nor the wrong man for the job. That something is very important to us doesn't make it a matter of morality, anymore than what Boozer is, is affected by what we think Boozer is.)

Although haunting questions are not easily dismissed, and may never be dismissed to the satisfaction of all, they can be put to rest for all practical purposes by an accumulation of evidence. This I shall attempt to do in the second half of this chapter by trying to destroy all other moral systems (religion, intuition, utilitarianism, fundamental rights, and reverence for life)—systems that are spurious in that most of them claim responsibility for the PC (but are not responsible) and are extremely dangerous if taken seriously because they all make demands in the name of morality (e.g., no compromise), yet they don't even direct their own adherents to the same conclusion on secondary-code acts (e.g., two intutionists may reach opposite conclusions on gambling).

I believe that if man had only recognized the true, ultimate, and all-but-universal guide for the proscription of certain acts, he would quickly have realized that no other guide gives clear direction to everyone, but also that the true ultimate guide *simply fails to guide on a lot of other acts*, and he would have faced what has, in fact, always been his true situation with regard to *all* other acts— namely, that he must form opinion about whether or not to allow these other acts. (What would guide individuals on these other acts and how conflicting opinions could be settled, I will explore further on.) But this he did not do, and the cost has been extraordinarily high.

What he did was place anything important to him at a specific time under the heading of morality, which instantly made millions of people in the world who had a different opinion immoral. When it comes to morality—or anything perceived as morality— there is, to repeat, no room for compromise (if we compromise with an arsonist, we burn), and indeed the immoral must be killed, segregated, or otherwise punished. When it comes to morality we cannot sacrifice it to anything without a deep sense of guilt and betrayal, which for most of us is too heavy a burden to bear. But where the secondary code has not been distinguished from the PC (which is everywhere), *everyone* is immoral in someone else's eyes, and in today's ever-shrinking world with ever-greater weaponry, the danger that all these secondary-code rights and wrongs will smash into one another with the force of PC truth has grown alarmingly.

Most of us feel that we must not kill or harm other people or sanction such policies unless we are morally right and they are morally wrong. Practically everyone knows that we simply cannot kill, segregate, or otherwise punish the innocent; but we must kill, segregate, or otherwise punish the guilty, and practically everyone knows *that*. But in the world we have created out of our linguistic confusion, where the two codes pass as one, everyone is a candidate for punishment. If we don't shed some of our righteousness by unlinking the two codes, we are all going to be killed.

Though I am troubled by the long odds against changing the common misusage of the language, I also believe, or hope, that if I can show that opinion and politics, far from being disreputable, are essential to life (if I can elevate opinion and politics to their rightful place alongside truth and morality, so that no one—except for the charlatan—sacrifices anything by labeling his or her opinions and politics for what they are, and risks a lot by not doing so), then perhaps the odds against changing common misusage may lessen somewhat. If, furthermore, I can show how individuals and groups reach secondary-code positions when they lose faith in the possibility of an ultimate guide; if I can show that theologians, intuitionists, utilitarians, humanists, animal lovers, liberals, conservatives, and decent and innocent people everywhere who say that gambling (or abortion or homosexuality or capital punishment or vivisection, etc.) is right or wrong don't know what they are talking about; and finally, if I can show that linking the two codes has been nothing less than mankind's most tragic mistake—then the odds against changing common misusage may lessen still more as we come to correct those who are misusing the moral hybrid form and laugh at the incorrigible as the literate have always laughed at the solecisms of the illiterate. I am not sanguine, but I am less sanguine that mankind can much longer tolerate secondary-code opinions held as moral truth.

TOLERANCE TOWARD OPINION

When we are faced with a decision involving others, but lack a generally shared desire or verifiable proposition to guide us, then we cannot form hybrids, and when we cannot form hybrids we are in the area of opinion. When we are talking opinion and *know* we are, tolerance and good feeling generally prevail, and are reflected in the words and phrases we use—"perhaps," "maybe," "who knows," "I don't know," "it's not a matter of right and wrong," "it's a political question," "it's open to compromise," "you can't win 'em all," "let's put it to a vote," etc.,—words and phrases that serve as linguistic signals that the matter can be settled one way or another without threatening anything ultimate. But because truth is essential to life and to living (arsenic *is* a poison; murder *is* wrong) and because opinion is different from truth, we have somehow got it in our heads that opinion is not important, which is probably the key reason we try to force so much of our opinion into the mold of truth. We have this same negative attitude toward politics and compromise as opposed to morality and principles—i.e., elevating the latter concepts over the former concepts. In fact, however, opinion, politics, and compromise are all essential if there is to be life—we cannot survive without them. Let me elaborate:

PROCESSING CONFLICTING OPINION

The desire that everything not be destroyed compels (1) the primary code and (2) that we do something with violators. However, this shared desire (this ultimate and all-but-universal guide) is silent on *what* to do with violators. Consequently, we have a moral question—a question that morality *demands* an answer to—but there is no *one* logical answer, no one moral truth as to what to do with violators that we can derive, logically, from the ultimate guide that nearly all of us share. Thus, even in the most rudimentary group, we must, of absolute necessity, form opinion. (And, in truth, opinion has always been sharply divided on what to do with violators, but not on the need to do *something*.) However, we cannot kill or assault one another over our different opinions, for this would destroy the group. Observe, then, the box we are in: We have, of absolute necessity, certain rudimentary decisions to make (some form of punishment); there is no true or logical answer; but there must be *an* answer, and we must not kill or assault one another in reaching it. In short, we must do something, but everyone may have a different idea of what to do, and indeed feel very strongly about his or her own idea.

The solution is what might be called a "process criterion" (a processor of conflicting opinions), or put in more familiar terms, a governmental or political system. Plato listed five possible systems of this kind, ranging from one "decider" (tyranny) to having all decide (democracy), but there are, in truth, many possibilities and variations. Melvin Konner speculates on man's first method for deciding conflicting opinion:

> Conflicts within the group are resolved by talking, sometimes half or all the night, for nights, weeks on end. After two years with the San, I came to think of the Pleistocene epoch of human history (the three million years during which we evolved) as one interminable marathon encounter group. When we slept in a grass hut in one of their villages, there were many nights when its flimsy walls leaked charged exchanges from the circle around the fire, frank expressions of feeling and contention beginning when the dusk fires were lit and running on until dawn.*

Whatever the method of deciding—whatever the political system—it will invariably answer other questions that members of the group may raise, apart from questions of kinds of punishment, and settle differences of opinion (e.g., whether to hire a night watchperson or continue to take turns guarding; whether to build a bridge or a ferry or neither; whether to drive on the left or the right side of the road; what the tax rate should be; etc.), none of which is logically compelled to be answered one way or another given the ultimate guide, or even a generally shared desire or verifiable proposition.

The Tangled Wing (New York: Holt, Rinehart & Winston, 1982), p. 7.

This process criterion; this decider of conflicting opinions; this political system (when it is working and generally accepted) *is more important to the individual* than his or her desire to have a bridge or a ferry, or a night watchperson, or a particular tax rate. The individual compromises his or her opinions on these matters (and even accepts defeat) for the sake of a higher-order desire *that the system prevail*, and be allowed to process the dozens, hundreds, or thousands of questions that are raised, the answers to which are not logically compelled by morality or even a shared desire within the group. *However*, if we believe our position on a particular question is *the correct moral answer*, then we cannot compromise without betraying morality, a betrayal that for most of us is too heavy a burden even to contemplate bearing, since buried in all the mess that passes for morality is always the PC and true morality. But the point now is only that we do in fact recognize a lot of opinion for what it is, and thus we let the political system decide—acrimonious as the debates may be.

Broadly speaking, as far as morality is concerned, a legitimate political system or government is one that abides by and fairly enforces the PC—a point I will expand upon as we go along. And morality demands that there be some form of political system to reach the opinions that must be reached in the administration of the PC. Some observations and explanations on the argument above:

• There is *moral truth*: truth logically compelled by the ultimate guide. Some of this truth is substantive (murder is wrong), some of it is procedural (bearing false witness is wrong) and, indeed, anything that is a clear threat to morality (including our misconceptions of the nature of morality) is wrong.

• There is also *moral opinion*. When morality demands that something be done (demands that killers be punished) but does not compel precisely what should be done, we must form opinion, and since more than one answer can satisfy morality, we can come up not with *the* answer but only with *an* answer. Thus, lest there be confusion, we must put our particular answer or our rejection of some other answer in the opinion form, e.g., "In *my opinion* capital punishment is wrong." The question of punishment is difficult enough to settle without, by implication, accusing the other side of being blind, crazy, or demonic, which it would be if it were advocating something that was truly wrong (e.g., wanting to let killers go free). *Moral opinion* comes about because morality demands an answer but doesn't give us the answer, and thus the question must be decided by the political system—which is to say we are facing both a moral and a political question.

• A *strictly political question* is one that doesn't have to be faced at all as far as morality is concerned, e.g., the question of whether gambling or alcohol should be prohibited. Questions like this are purely political, or if no one raises them, they are simply "free choices" according to society at large.

• Practically any act could fall under the heading of morality if "enormous numbers" of people did it excessively. Gambling and drinking could become moral questions if everyone drank and gambled all day, every day. However, *fear* of enormous numbers (if we allow people to do certain acts) and actual enormous numbers are two different things, and the failure to make the distinction has caused endless problems in moral discourse; this, too, we shall see further on. Sometimes, however, we truly are faced with "enormous numbers," and sometimes morality gives the precise answer: In the sixties, given the enormous amount of radiation released into the atmosphere by above-ground nuclear testing (and the enormous numbers of people potentially affected), we faced a form of pollution that was clearly immoral, and in fact the major powers stopped such testing for this very reason. Clearly those countries that continue to test above ground are committing an immoral act.

• Beyond telling the innocent what they must do to survive— i.e., put away killers (etc.)—morality has nothing else to say to them, and simply does not guide on a lot of extremely difficult questions that the innocent face, questions that traditionally (and mistakenly) have been called moral. The fact that a question is a matter of life or death does not make it moral. For example, short of "enormous numbers" of women having an abortion everytime they become pregnant, morality is silent on abortion, for nearly everyone involved is innocent—legislators, pregnant women, fetuses.* Indeed, the only ones not innocent are the passionate moralists on both sides of the issue, for by claiming that the issue is moral and that their answer is *the* moral answer they are confusing the true nature of morality and are, therefore, a threat to morality. This threat can become a reality—with legitimate political systems torn apart and great amounts of blood shed over "moral" questions that are not moral questions.

• This raises a further question. Since so many people perceive nonmoral acts as matters of morality, why, then, are not all political systems in a state of chronic and bloodletting disorder? The answer is what might be called "the moral ambivalence of the neutral middle," those generally large numbers of people who, while confused about the true nature of morality, somehow find reasons *not* to kill and punish one another over every question that wins the imprimatur of "morality," and who fear the passionate moralists, even though they may envy them for their "strong convictions." What I am trying to say is that the very vice of the "neutral middle" is its true virtue. But far too often those in the middle, confused as to the true nature of morality, come to believe that they have a moral choice to make—they ask, "Is abortion right or wrong?" rather than, "Is it neither?"—since the ultimate guide fails to give clear direction. Instead, those in the middle get trapped in the argument, split along the question, and then feel that they cannot compromise or accept defeat without being immoral. Worst of all, in these far-too-frequent situations, no political leader dares say that the issue is not a matter of morality but a matter of opinion to be settled by the political system in the normal manner, for this would infuriate both sides. Instead, political leaders call on

---

*In societies that do not know about birth control or abortion, infanticide has sometimes been practiced, and horrible as it is to contemplate, it is not necessarily immoral, if the *true* alternative to it is the death of adults and other children by starvation. Morality just cannot guide when some innocent must die in either case—which is why such questions are so difficult.

the black/white language of morality, thus confirming the false assumptions of both sides that the issue is one of truth, and the leaders—now fearing for their political lives—easily work themselves into a passion equal to that of moralists. If the followers understood things differently, the leaders would talk differently; and the followers would understand things differently, if the leaders would talk differently . . . but then they wouldn't be leaders. What we must say to the passionate moralist is: "Give us your opinion, sit down, shut up, and let the political process prevail." But we seldom say this, for who would dare talk this way to someone "honestly speaking from his or her deepest convictions"? (Am I making light of the moralists' position? Hardly, I am scared to death of it, and them.) The one word that if slipped into all this chaos would tell us exactly where we are, namely, "opinion," is taboo in serious discussion. We are sailors who have banned the compass.

The answer to the question "How would a group decide secondary-code questions if it no longer believed them to be moral?" is "The same way it is now settling questions it does not believe to be moral." There are no particular problems for a group in unlinking the two codes; it is when they are linked that they can tear a group apart, as each side is unable to compromise or accept defeat. A people can decide to divide, and each go his or her own way; a legitimate political system can be torn down and a new one established; and an immoral political system *must* be changed or torn down—but the reasoning must be correct if those doing the tearing down or changing are not themselves to be guilty of immorality. The most incorrect reasoning of all is to tear apart, change, punish, and kill in the name of a secondary-code interest that passes as morality.

• Morality's silence on such secondary-code acts as gambling, alcohol, and abortion also means that *there is no moral reason* that these acts cannot be proscribed (we are given a "free choice" even as to whether to proscribe them or not), and since they can be proscribed, then violators can (legitimately) be punished, for proscriptions without punishments are just maxims. In short, *legitimate political systems can proscribe and punish acts other than the PC acts.* However, morality insists that none of these other acts may be proscribed in the name of morality, for this confuses morality's true nature and is a threat to morality. Two final and related points: the Law (a group's PC and non-PC laws) must be fair and administered fairly, for anything else means that a person (e.g., a tyrant) or subgroup (the police) is in a position of determining who should be punished and who should not based on personal prejudice or interests. And this means, in effect, a breakdown between guilt and innocence, which invariably leads to a breakdown in the administration of the PC itself, and a society led by the most destructive. (A prime example of this is, of course, racist laws, which are now correctly viewed as immoral. They do threaten the destruction of everything, as we can imagine ever-smaller groups making ever-finer racial distinctions until it is the end of us—a French Revolution of racial purity as it were. More on this point further on.)

• The demands of the PC aside (that there be a political system for settling certain moral questions and for administering the PC), a political system and its *non-PC laws* are terribly important, *for they establish the very quality of life for their people.* While a society that allows prostitution, homosexuality, abortion, premarital sex, gambling, pornography, alcohol, birth-control devices, and free expression is not morally superior to one that forbids all these acts, the two societies are obviously *very different*, and one's opinions on these matters are, consequently, very important. But the point is that simply because a question is important, it is not necessarily moral, and to call it moral is dangerous, for we confuse the true nature of morality and close the door to compromise even as we open the door to a bloodbath of moral righteousness.

In summary, if morality had a voice, its words would be like the harsh, egocentric, narrow-minded, and even cruel words of the God of the Old Testament: "I am what I am and am nothing else. Put nothing before me. I care nothing for most of your concerns, except that I see these concerns gripping you so much that you put them before me and carelessly throw away your lives killing others in my name. You are an abomination to me when you use my name when I have not spoken. You give yourselves rights and say I gave them to you; you forbid your neighbors from doing this and that and say I forbid it—I gave you *nothing* but the PC and I forbid *nothing* but the PC acts, and if you do not stop these offenses against me, you will die."

REACHING ONE'S PERSONAL POSITION
ON SECONDARY-CODE ACTS

How would a person reach his or her secondary-code position if he or she lost faith in the possibility of an ultimate criterion for guidance? The answer, as we might expect by now, is the same way he or she reaches a position on any matter that is not perceived as moral.

Consider the question of the tax rate: Morality demands a political system, and practically any form of political system demands some form of taxation. But while the tax rate can be of direct concern to morality (if it is so high that it denies some people the basics of life), most of the time the rate is recognized as a political question and people realize that opinion is needed to set an appropriate rate, since there is no *true and just* rate written in stone somewhere.

I have said earlier that I do not know how the human mind actually forms opinion, but that there can be no conscious opinion-forming unless we recognize first that we are in the area of opinion and not truth. (This is a question that can be determined objectively— do we have a verifiable proposition that *this* decision holds the best chance of satisfying a generally shared desire? If we do not, we are in the area of opinion.) In any case, it would seem that in a democracy, at least, some people are comfortably guided to their position on the tax rate by narrow self-interest; some by liberal or conservative principles that they believe will bring about the kind of society they would most like to live in; some by their concern for inflation, interest rates, social programs, or military preparedness; some by their sense of fairness—and most of us by a combination of these and other factors. But most of us acknowledge that there is no *one* answer and that we, as individuals, are therefore excused (by morality) from finding it. Even though we may be considerably troubled if our position does not prevail, we are usually more troubled at the prospect of destroying our political system over the question, which means that we know we must compromise our position and even accept defeat.

The point of all this is that individuals now have their methods for reaching their personal positions on political questions, and that even though these methods do not come up with *the* answer, they do, collectively, come up with *an* answer to political questions. Indeed, some people (including, no doubt, many politicians) are already using what is in effect a *nonmoral method* for reaching their personal positions on some of the most tortured secondary-code questions they face. For example, leaving aside those who claim to *know* that abortion is morally wrong, and those who claim to *know* that abortion is every woman's basic right, it is also true that some people are frankly forming opinion on the abortion question and know they are, and are frankly looking for a solution that they can best live with. Many politicians may feel they can best live with whatever decision holds the best promise of keeping them in office—a consideration not to be quickly dismissed in a democracy. But when other people say, as some do, "I have wrestled long and hard with the question, and while I find abortion to be repugnant, I just can't bring myself to force a woman to continue a pregnancy she does not want," it may be an honest reflection of an inner struggle. The same would go for "I know it is a terrible hardship for some women, but I just cannot see terminating human life once it has begun." Which is to say, we can still think about and decide on secondary-code questions, even if we exclude the black/white language of morality.

And one other point: While a lot has been said against totalitarian political systems, one of their advantages is that they settle secondary-code questions without endless debate, a debate that some societies simply cannot afford to spend any time on, given the pressing demand to plant, cultivate, and harvest.

I am certain that there will be many sane and sensible people who will say that I don't *really mean* that the PC is all there is to morality, or that if I insist that I do, I am simply confused. They will contend that *true* morality is a rich, complex business that can't be reduced to a simple formula. To which I respond: Make more of morality than it is, and you are going to destroy us all in this ever-shrinking world with ever-greater weaponry. We simply cannot stand still when people are acting immorally, but if we make more of morality than it is, then we have a world in which people won't stand still for anything. This, I believe, is the actual world we have created out of our linguistic confusion. The linking of the two codes has been nothing less, I believe, than mankind's most tragic mistake. I have acknowledged that the odds against unlinking the two codes are long, but maybe if we see how the mistake came to be made—leading to ever-higher body counts in the name of right—more and more people may be frightened enough or embarrassed enough not to continue making the mistake and to slip the word "opinion" into statements where it properly belongs—and laugh at those who don't.

HOW THE TWO CODES BECAME LINKED

Secondary-code proscriptions were, no doubt, often incorporated into a group's Code by an argument from an unannounced metaphor.* Thus, at some time in some group (let me call it group Alpha, and let us assume that Alpha is isolated from knowledge of all other groups) a man, in a state of rage because his mate lost the family possessions gambling, might have cried out, "Gambling is robbery; it is wrong." At this moment the members of the group probably made the mistake of asking one another, "Is gambling *really* wrong?" when the initial question should have been, "Wrong in terms of what?" The answer to the latter question may show (and indeed does show in the case of gambling) that allowing

---

*Arguments from unannounced metaphors continue even today, when we hear it said, for example, "Abortion is murder and therefore wrong." That this statement is, at heart, a metaphor becomes apparent when those making it usually acknowledge, if pressed, that they don't want the electric chair or life imprisonment for the guilty. Abortion may be likened to murder for dramatic effect, but if it were murder then not only would the penalty have to be the same as for murder, abortion would have to be considered murder in the first degree, since by its very nature it is premeditated.

or forbidding the act is neither right nor wrong given a generally shared desire and a verifiable proposition—the prerequisites necessary to form a hybrid—but rather, gambling is a matter of opinion, and this would make the question of how a group should regard gambling substantively different from the question of how the group should regard robbery. But there is no evidence that this distinction was ever made by any ancient tribe, and let's assume that the Alphans didn't make it either. The point I am trying to make here is that however Alpha referred to the PC acts, that is exactly how it talked about secondary-code acts, which was a mistake, since the two acts are substantively different.

Depending on the allies the troubled man was able to muster and the reaction of the leaders (perhaps whether they themselves liked to gamble), gambling might have been proscribed and the proscriptions incorporated into Alpha's Code. Let us assume that Alpha did proscribe gambling and called it wrong, but that it did not proscribe wine; indeed, wine is worshipped. (The reason I have them drinking wine will be apparent in a moment.)

Now, the mistake that Alpha made (in not recognizing that gambling and robbery are two substantively different acts) is not a serious mistake as long as Alpha is isolated from knowledge of all other tribes and as long as just about everyone in Alpha accepts its Code, which is to say, in effect, that just about everyone *is of the opinion* that gambling should be proscribed. In short, the tribal grammar works, and there are no particular problems created by the linguistic convention of calling secondary-code acts wrong.

Nevertheless, Alpha's use of language raises an interesting question, namely, what do we have and how should we properly express it when *everyone* holds the same opinion? Truly universal opinion is rare but not unknown—public nudity and cannibalism are two examples. Assuming the weather is mild, there is nothing wrong with public nudity given a generally shared desire *and* a verifiable proposition, but most everyone is of the opinion (and desires) that some clothing be worn in public. Nor is there anything wrong with eating one's slain enemies given some generally shared desire and a verifiable proposition, but now most everyone finds it distasteful.

Here it would seem that we enter a linguistic twilight zone, for to say "In my opinion . . ." or "In our opinion . . ." X is wrong implies that there is other opinion around, which is not the case. Yet, to say "X is wrong" gives us the hybrid form, which implies there is a hybrid argument behind the statement, but this is not the case either for there is, for example, no verifiable proposition involved. However, because these opinions are all-but-universally shared we have something far more powerful than ordinary opinion, and however we state it, our statement is as powerful as any hybrid, for at the heart of the matter is the same thing that is at the heart of a hybrid statement—namely, a shared desire. These shared desires (on nudity and cannibalism) are not logically derived from some higher-order and generally shared desire, but are—like the desire to live—basic and unsupported. We can get a feel for this if we are confronted by a would-be suicide, or a man who wants to run naked in the streets, or a cannibal. We may plead or rage or display our revulsion, and in the case of the naked man and the cannibal we may threaten, but a logically compelling argument seems beyond our grasp.* What we have here are all-but-universally shared desires versus the singular desires of would-be nudists and cannibals, but desires versus desires nevertheless, with no transcendent and shared desire to appeal to, and thus no logically compelling argument to be made. This does not mean that in the case of the naked man and the cannibal, an all-but-absolute majority is suddenly powerless, any more than it is powerless in the case of a killer, for we can and do force our desires on them.

That might makes our right is something we do not like to acknowledge and it is one reason that morality has become so mystified. We want to win the naked man and the cannibal over by

---

*I am not saying that people don't give reasons against public nudity and cannibalism from a criterion, but only that the criterion is not universally shared, or it raises more questions than it answers, e.g., cannibalism and public nudity are uncivilized, but what do you mean by uncivilized? etc. That we do not have a compelling argument, however, doesn't matter, for we do have a generally shared desire (no public nudity, no cannibalism) and, for the most part, we don't need an argument since there is no one to argue with. As to the question of how we should express truly universal opinion, that, too, doesn't matter much and the tribal convention of calling what everyone doesn't want "wrong" will get us by without trouble.

rational argument, or condemn them by something other than our desire, but alas there is no transcendent argument to be made; there is only us, and our desires, versus them and their desires.

One final point about universal opinion that may help to put the nature of morality in sharper focus. The question may arise as to why cannibalism and public nudity are not matters of morality, since nearly everyone is against them. The answer is that our desires against these acts are not always ultimate considerations: given the choice of burning to death or running naked in the street, not burning to death is the higher consideration and is accepted by all but the most prudish as the higher consideration. And given the choice of starving to death or eating the dead, not starving to death would be the higher consideration for many people.

Returning now to group Alpha: We have assumed that it is isolated from knowledge of all other tribes, which is to say that it is its own universe. Thus, its secondary code (assuming it is generally accepted) is a set of "universal" opinions and shared desires (that certain acts not be done) and one of these opinions is that gambling be forbidden. Thus the statement "Gambling is wrong" is much more than an opinion or a false hybrid, rather it is the direct expression of a generally shared desire. And, as a linguistic convention, the statement "Gambling is wrong" works perfectly well in tribe Alpha, even though the statement is not a hybrid. And, in truth, even the gamblers in tribe Alpha (if there are any) probably take their inclination to be immoral, since Alpha's Code is its Code, with no distinction recognized between one wrong (e.g., arson) and another wrong (e.g., gambling).

It is possible to imagine Alpha getting along successfully for centuries enjoying its wine, often to excess, while parents teach and children accept that, among other things, arson and gambling are both wrong. But the more certain and steady Alpha's Code, the graver the trauma when it comes across another tribe, Omega, with another code, where *alcohol is strictly forbidden* but gambling is not only allowed but popular. *Once Alpha makes contact with Omega, the linguistic convention of calling gambling morally wrong will cause horrendous problems for both groups.* Or, looked at another way, a minor mistake (calling secondary-code opinion morally wrong) becomes a major mistake when Alpha makes contact with Omega.

Let us concentrate on Alpha. Not only will Alpha fear and hate Omega for its blatant "immorality," it will be faced with grave doubts—could Omega be right and Alpha wrong? Since its two codes are one in the confused minds of the members of Alpha, what will come into question will not be the authority for its secondary-code proscriptions but the authority for *all* it holds right and wrong (including the PC, for even though Omega also proscribes murder, etc., the question that has arisen is the basic metaethical question: "Why is *anything* right or wrong and how do we know?"). Anarchy and relativism seem right around the corner; Alpha, viewing Omega (and vice versa), will feel a sudden and dreadful loss of support for its basic beliefs. This trauma—this sudden exposure to the basic metaethical question—has been, historically, very real, as I am about to show. It is at this point, feeling under tremendous pressure, that we find what can only be called mankind's most dreadful mistake: a tragic answer (to the metaethical question) that is still with us in many places even today and is still (tragically) shaping the course of human history.

THE TRAGIC ANSWER

While Pleistocene man may have segregated and tabooed those who committed certain acts because of fear of a spirit world, by the time of the earliest Egyptians and Babylonians in the fifth millennium B.C., all linkage between the Codes of these early societies and the supernatural had disappeared. Their gods were fertility gods, and "least of all did the worshippers of such a god [Re, the Egyptian god of the sun] conceive of him as having any ideas of right or wrong, or any desire to lay such requirements upon his worshippers, who considered themselves as expected only to present certain propitiatory offerings just as they might present them to a local chieftain."*

The list of dos and don'ts that guided the earliest Egyptians had no recognized foundation—or at least the pharaohs, demigods themselves, were authority enough—and the basic metaethical

---

*James Henry Breasted, *The Dawn of Conscience* (New York: Scribner's, 1933), p. 81.

question ("How do we know our Code is the right Code?") was unasked and therefore unanswered. Like the Nile, morality flowed on, timeless, ineluctable, and unquestioned.

But along the way, in each society, something happened. Specifically, God was brought into morality, sometimes gradually and sometimes boldly at a point in history. The reason seems clear, namely, to answer the basic metaethical question. While trade, migration, and invasion, which put conflicting Codes in contact with one another, no doubt had a lot to do with raising the metaethical question, in the case of the Egyptians the pressure to answer it seems to have been gradual.

In 4000 B.C. we have the locution "he who does what is loved" for the innocent. Later we have the word *Maat* that has been translated as "righteousness." Now in the twenty-eighth century B.C., according to Breasted, one of the official names of King Userkaf was "Doer of Righteousness (Maat)." A hundred years later Ptahhotep—an adviser to the pharaoh Isesis—set down a list of maxims for his son, who was about to begin a career in government, and said, "I have attained one hundred and ten years of life, while the king gave to me rewards above [those of] the ancestors because I *did righteousness* [*Maat*] for the king even unto the grave."* All of which indicates that up to this point *Maat*, was something in the hearts and minds of kings, bureaucrats, and ordinary citizens. There was no mention that it might exist anywhere else.

Ptahhotep's maxims were probably as hackneyed then as they are today: "Be not proud of thy learning," "Let thy mind be deep and thy speech scanty." But suddenly there is a tremendous surprise, at least for us, and maybe for Ptahhotep's son and others who read his document:

> It is the understanding (literally "heart") which makes its possessor a hearkener or one not hearkening. The good fortune of a man is his understanding. How worthy it is when a son hearkens to his father! If the son of man receives what his father says, none of his projects

---

*Breasted, op. cit., p. 129.

will miscarry . . . how many mishaps befall him who hearkens not
. . . A *hearkener is one whom the god loves, one whom the god hates is one
who hearkens not.* [Emphasis added.]*

Amazing! The old man has tied up his wisdom in a bundle
and marked it as coming from a god. What son would now dare
not hearken? No longer does Re circle the earth oblivious to man's
doings—he is concerned! He loves and hates how the man and
child behave. It would now be only a matter of time until *Maat*
(righteousness) became the primary attribute of the sun god; until
what one did in this life mattered in the next; and until the
Egyptians moved to monotheism.† The importance of monotheism seems clear, for without it the metaethical question would
remain—which god is the right god? But monotheism also requires
the possibility of conversion, for without it most people in the
world would be "immoral," adhering as they do to other Codes
dictated by false gods. From here it is but a step or two away from
forced conversions, crusades, inquisitions, and attacks against "em-
pires of evil."

In other societies God was brought in less subtly to support
morality. Compared with other moral codes, the Babylonian Code
—and the laws and punishments it sanctioned—was particularly
harsh on the poor and the landless, and troubling questions were
being asked of the established order. But Hammurabi (1750 B.C.)
answered them: he went into the desert, and when he came back
he announced that he had received a code from Marduk, the most
popular of the Babylonian gods. While this revealed code established fixed penalties for the first time (a reform), on everything
else Marduk confirmed *the existing Babylonian law and morality.* The
basic metaethical question was answered, the Babylonian Code was
the right Code, and the rest of the world was wrong and immoral.
Breaches of morality and the law were now not only wrong and
illegal, they were affronts to God.

Moses (1450 B.C.) was faced with a more immediate political

---

*Breasted, op. cit., p. 130.

†Ibid., pp. 144-46.

problem, but his solution was similar. He went to the mountain to get the word from God and, *with one revealing exception*, came back with the obvious—namely, the very code the Jews were already living by, for prior to his going the Jews were not killing and stealing with impunity, nor had there been a sudden outbreak of adultery and false witness. The one exception was a secondary-code question of extreme importance to Moses at the time—namely, *the question of graven images*. Not only were such images sanctioned in other societies, but Aaron, Moses' chief rival among the Jews, had started making them, contrary to Jewish tradition, and had attracted a considerable following. Who was right and who was wrong? Moses went to the mountain and came back with the answer in writing—no graven images; Aaron and the rest of the world were wrong, for this was the word of the one true God.

Moses' triumph over Aaron was an astonishing piece of work, for if Aaron said the tablets did not come from God, he was then in the awkward position of having to acknowledge that Moses was a wise man, as there was no doubt among the Jews that most of the Ten Commandments were true. But if Aaron allowed that Moses was the messenger of God, he was then in the position of disobeying the word of God concerning graven images. In fact, Aaron and "his sons the priests" were undone, and if we turn to the far more detailed Hebrew version of the Pentateuch, we find Moses now in firm command and giving the Jews scores of secondary-code proscriptions on the most minute matters, all of which he said he received from God.

But what a tragic answer God was to the basic metaethical question—and what a mistake for mankind not to recognize the difference between the PC truth and secondary-code opinion. Because then man would have realized that *everybody* is right, for everybody has the PC, though people may differ on questions that are not moral. With the two codes linked and with both now linked to God, even the slightest violation of the Code of one's own group was an insult to the absolute, and when it comes to the absolute, there is no such thing as a slight insult. Indeed, the secondary-code proscriptions took on tremendous importance, for violators were taken to be saying, "I follow the god of another group—the god of strangers, foreigners, and those who live in moral squalor" (e.g., Sodomites). And much of the skull-crushing *within* groups was over what to an outsider might seem to be a minor matter—drinking some fermented grapes or rolling some dice across the floor—but such was the fear that violators were disloyal to the Code and the group, that the most insignificant matter might easily become a test for loyalty. Too, there was always the legitimate concern that *any* attempt to question the Code might lead to relativism and anarchy, for buried in everyone's Code is the PC.

Much of the skull-crushing *between* groups has always been in the name of the one true morality and the one true God. Once the one true God put his stamp of approval on a secondary-code belief, everyone who didn't hold this belief became instantly immoral, and the immoral, as we know, must be punished. With secondary-code proscriptions now linked to the absolute, people who once solved their conflicting opinions by endlessly "talking through the night" (as the San still do) could no longer talk, since when it comes to absolutes there is no room for compromise, and therefore nothing to talk about.

The question at hand is not whether God exists, nor which prophet is the true prophet. *The question concerns what I have called the theological fallacy*, for if we didn't know right from wrong *in the first place*, we wouldn't know God from the Devil if we fell over Him. If all there were to what passes for morality was the PC, voices from beyond would be hopelessly redundant; if all there were to morality were the secondary codes, we would long ago have realized it couldn't have been God we heard, but the Devil himself, for who but the Devil would give so many conflicting instructions? But with both codes passing as morality, we were confused and frightened at the prospect of relativism; God got into morality and, to say the least, is still not out. To say that we must have faith that the voice we heard was the voice of God means, in effect, that we must have faith to know that murder, arson, assault, and robbery are wrong—which is absurd. And all this means that Ayatollah Khomeini, Jerry Falwell, Billy Graham, Reverend Moon, and Pope John Paul II are either dreadfully confused about the nature of right and wrong or are charlatans, and in either case must be dismissed when they tell us *anything* about behavior from their official position. When Reverend Moon tells us he talks with God everyone laughs, but papal authority is founded on a book full of such claims, so the laughter must become infectious—for the big problem we face is not that peace doesn't have enough spokespersons (among which, I grant, the Pope is a leader) but that religion in the realm of politics and morality leads to war and may kill us all.

There is, I believe, a place for religion in our lives—to aid the afflicted and to get us through the dark nights of the soul—but when it comes to how we should act, these men and women in cloth are privy to no inside information and the sooner they stop taking advantage of us (and the sooner we stop allowing them to take advantage of us) the safer the world will be.

THE INTUITIONIST'S FALLACY

In trying to come up with some answer other than God to the basic metaethical question, philosophers have failed, and indeed their answers would have proven just as dangerous as God had any of them attracted a wide following. Let me now take up some of the major arguments, expose their errors, and point out the inherent dangers.

"Writers who maintain that we have 'intuitive knowledge' of the rightness of actions usually mean that this rightness is ascertained by simply 'looking at' the actions themselves, without considering their ulterior consequences."* This is the intuitionists' position, any list of whom would probably include Henry Sidgwick, G. E. Moore, C. D. Broad, A. C. Ewing and W. D. Ross.

Intuition is seductive in that it takes credit for that jolt of truth we all get for the PC hybrids, and in its elegant disdain for *reasoning*. When a friend has been killed by a mugger, who cares for reasoning? Such an act is wrong, here and now, in and of itself, and to bring in reasons for the wrongness of the act—to have to explain its wrongness—is, we feel, an affront to the memory of our friend and

---

*Henry Sidgwick, *The Methods of Ethics* (London: Macmillan, 1874; New York: Dover, 1966), p. 96 of the Dover edition.

to the terribleness of the deed. Nevertheless, intuition fails completely on secondary-code questions and is guilty of a fallacy that destroys its credibility even with regard to the PC acts. Let me begin with the fallacy:

Among intuitionists, I think it would be fair to say that all hold certain acts (murder, arson, robbery, etc.) to be wrong, but on other acts (gambling, abortion, capital punishment) there is disagreement. Clearly, if intuition is our ultimate source of moral knowledge, then some intuitionists are misreading their intuitions some of the time, since some say a given act is right (or a right) while others say it is wrong, and the same act cannot be both. Some may say they know, intuitively, that a particular act is neither right nor wrong—but this merely gives us a third category and further disagreement. If intuition is held to be the ultimate foundation of morality, then either intuition is contradictory (and worthless) or some people are mistaken some of the time.

If mistakes about our intuitions are possible, how do we know when they are being made? For that matter, how do we know that every intuitionist isn't wrong about murder, arson, and robbery? If the intuitionist argues that when everyone has the same intuition then we know we are right, I must ask, "How do you know this?" At this point the intuitionist must either bring in some other criterion for support (e.g., the preservation of society), in which case intuition is not ultimate, or he must say, "I just know it," in which case he is asking his method to support itself—a fatal error. In either case, it seems to me, the intuitionist is undone.

If all there were to what is called morality was the PC, we would long ago have discovered that the desire that life go on gave us these basic proscriptions *and* the intuitive feel (or jolt of truth, if I may) that these acts are wrong. If all there were to what is called morality were the secondary codes, then intuition would long ago have been exposed as patently worthless, since it misdirects half of its followers all the time. But with the two codes passing as one, and with everyone getting the same intuitive jolt that certain acts are wrong, intuition has always had a certain cachet about it (as do most of the major theories, inasmuch as they, too, give us the PC). Nevertheless, as a means of guidance, intuition is superfluous where it appears to work and dangerous where it does not. It is trouble enough that we disagree on certain acts without putting the full faith and credit of morality behind the intuitive feel of both sides. As to the haunting question "Can't something be morally wrong even if it is not wrong given the desire to live and maintain a group?" the answer is a definite no, if what is haunting us is our intuition. For if you are haunted one way and I am haunted another way on a given question, intuition is useless for settling it, and we had better quickly move on to some other criterion (e.g., a process criterion) if we don't want to end up assaulting or killing one another in a fit of moral righteousness.

In real life, intuition is a very dangerous business, for it is often called upon as the foundation of certain general rules and maxims, rules and maxims that when taken as morality, in which no compromise is possible, can lead to disaster. But when we realize that these rules and maxims are actually founded on the kind of group most of us desire to live in, namely, a group where people return things they have borrowed, keep their promises, meet their obligations, don't lie and cheat, and treat others as they would like to be treated themselves, then we also realize that these rules and maxims are *not* morality but are subordinate to it, for they *must* be set aside when following them will bring about disaster (e.g., returning a machine gun to a mad killer just because it happens to be his). Those who stick by the rules although it causes death and destruction may feel good about themselves, but they are as immoral as murderers since they cause the death of innocents; they are rule worshippers, and as dangerous a lot as one is likely to run across in life.

KANT'S ERRORS

An opinion, as we have noted, can become a hybrid if "enormous numbers" are involved. If almost everyone spent his and her days in drunken gambling and his and her nights having sex only with those of the same sex, then that would be the end of us, and those demanding that we change our ways would be morally correct. However, an argument from "enormous numbers" is logically compelling only when there is a real likelihood of "enormous numbers" and disaster if we don't forbid an act. Or, looked at another way, worry about "enormous numbers" is not enough to give us moral truth and forbid an act on moral grounds. Nevertheless, arguments from this worry are fascinating, for in using them people are vaguely aware of the true foundation of morality, namely, the desire that life go on and that disaster be avoided.

Immanuel Kant and parents throughout history both argue in the same way: parents ask children, "What would happen if *everyone* did that?" and Kant gives us the categorical imperative—"Act only according to a maxim by which you can at the same time will it shall become general law." Broadly speaking, Kant is on to something, but he makes so many errors in reasoning that what he is on to gets lost. Most important, Kant fails to give us the basic assumption of his own argument.

What Kant doesn't tell us, but I assume he would tell us if he thought about it, is that if we make a general rule of our act *and* it leads to disaster (because everyone follows the rule), then the act is wrong and we ought not to do it. This means that avoiding disaster is our ultimate guide, and that the categorical imperative is only a dramatic way of finding out what leads to disaster (i.e., suppose everyone did this act).

Now, if Kant had only explored his own argument further (and developed the disaster guide), he would have been on to the true foundation of the PC proscriptions; he would have realized that his categorical imperative is dangerous to worthless in that, unqualified, it leads to the banning of far too many acts; and he would have realized that the question is not what would happen if *everyone* went around killing (etc.), but what would happen if *we* allowed *one* killer to go about his or her business.

This he did not do, and thus he did not come up with the true foundation of morality. Instead, he dangerously confused matters. Kant's argument puts an obligation on the killer not to kill, because if everyone did it, the result would be disaster. Mankind's true life-and-death situation is that we have got to get killers out of the way, regardless of what obligation they accept or don't accept. Kant opens the door to confusion where we dare not be confused—and God help us all if we take seriously a killer who has come up with *his* interpretation of Kant (e.g., that every killing ends a little suffering in the world).

On secondary-code acts, or *any act* a person can commit (for the categorical imperative makes no distinctions), Kant's argument is ridiculous. If each individual ponders his or her act according to Kant's imperative, then no one could go over the Brooklyn Bridge, for if everyone did it, it would lead to disaster. Yet, as weak as Kant's argument seems on its face, it has actually been invoked to support certain secondary-code proscriptions, such as those against homosexual acts.

Let me elaborate on this point: Moral philosophers have generally understood that the innocent are inviolable, for that is why they are in business in the first place, namely, to distinguish between right and wrong, guilt and innocence, and if the innocent are to be punished, too, then we don't have a guide that has any meaning, we just have people with power guided by personal prejudice. And this has led to the correct understanding that a moral system and the proscriptions it leads to will fall apart if exceptions are made in its enforcement.* If there is a proscription, there can be no exceptions under ordinary circumstances; and if there is no proscription, there can be no punishment under any circumstances.

Thus, if two homosexuals are allowed to go about their business (no proscription), then there is no (logical) way we can prevent a third, fourth, or fifth from joining them (since there is no proscription). And this has been generally understood. And so, too, with allowing gambling and drinking. By allowing anyone to commit these acts, we set a precedent. Setting precedents is clearly serious business and has, generally speaking, always been understood as serious business, for the way is now open for everyone to do any act that is not forbidden. At this point the possibility arises that enormous numbers of people will commit such acts if allowed to do them; people become frightened by the disaster this would

---

*This is true of any system, from a game to a political system. Football just won't survive if the referee can arbitrarily impose penalties, nor, I believe, will a political system long endure if law enforcement officials arrest and convict those they don't like. What I am trying to say is that blatant unfairness and injustice will, sooner or later, destroy any group or system.

bring about and, consequently, the acts are often proscribed. In such cases people are actually calling on the true foundation of morality, i.e., avoiding the destruction of everything. (They answer Mom, Dad, and Kant's question: If everyone did *that* it would lead to total disaster, and since I don't want that, it would be incoherent of me to do it or to allow anyone to do it.)

However, what is missing in such an argument is a verifiable proposition or at least some hard evidence that if we allow *one* person to drink, gamble, and have sex with someone of the same sex, we will have a society of drunken, homosexual gamblers whose acts will lead to the destruction of everything. Public policy must not be determined by considerations lacking such hard evidence, for if we start banning everything that would lead to disaster if everyone did it, we would end up with a hopeless number of proscriptions that must either be ignored (a dangerous precedent) or whose enforcement will crush society.

Here, then, is the solution to the problem of precedents: If there is no hard evidence that if we allow one person to do a particular act then everyone will want to do it *and* total disaster will follow, then we must reach our decision (on gambling, drinking, homosexual acts, etc.) on some other criterion than the end of the world. Those who argue from "enormous numbers" are taking morality into account, but morality insists that if the evidence does not reveal that the destruction of everything is truly at stake, then morality's name should be kept out of it.

To complicate matters, there are a number of acts (e.g., double-parking, paying taxes, jury duty) with respect to which, if some people were permitted to do as they pleased, virtually all people would do as they pleased (namely, not pay taxes, etc.), and this would lead to the breakdown of the political system. While there is nothing morally wrong with changing even a legitimate political system, one must have a political system, which probably requires taxation. The point is that, human nature being what it is, there are a lot of possibilities given a specific act: If we allow one person to do it, it can destroy everything; if we allow anyone to do it, everyone will do it; and, if we allow anyone to do it, only some will do it. Which is to say, among other things, that murder, homosexual behavior, and paying taxes are three very different matters and must be considered differently.

Once again the haunting question arises in one of its many forms: If we really are faced with enormous numbers but a lot of people don't or won't face these numbers, then are not those who want to take action to prevent or minimize the enormous numbers morally right and everyone else morally wrong? The answer is yes, for just as there are true scientific propositions that people did not or do not accept (that the earth is round, the Copernican theory that the planets travel around the sun, the theory of evolution), so, too, we can have true moral hybrids that not eveyone accepts, even though everyone shares the desire that life continue and no one can refute the compelling argument that supports the proscription in question.

We found this situation when scientists first concluded that continued use of chlorofluorocarbon would diminish the ozone layer in the atmosphere to such an extent that all life would be threatened. If we accept their evidence, the statement "Making and using chlorofluorocarbon is morally wrong" is true. Yet, for a time, a number of people in the chemical industry and related industries would not accept it; and during this time the answer to the haunting question was a definite yes—half the world can be morally right and half the world morally wrong. But in this case there was a compelling, verifiable propositon and it ground down those whose position was immoral. As I have noted before, we also had this situation with another form of intolerable pollution—namely, that caused by above-ground nuclear testing; my conclusion was that those who are still doing it are immoral.

When it comes to nuclear weapons in general, most people understand that we are faced with a moral question, but what many people do not seem to understand is that, unlike the case with the question of above-ground nuclear testing, morality compels no *one* answer (e.g., stop making the weapons immediately and destroy those we already have), since a build-down itself is a risky business, at least in the opinion of many other people, that could actually cause a nuclear war if it was not carefully carried out such that no one side had a sudden advantage over the other. Nuclear proliferation is a moral question, but morality is silent on the precise answer. Nevertheless, morality demands *an* answer, and in my opinion one of the things that stands in the way of *an* answer are the people with *the* answer, for they hold that anyone with a different answer from theirs is immoral, which is infuriating and delays everything. My own view, for what it is worth, is that if the anti-nuclear protestors would stop giving us the true answer and, instead, demand that the major political leaders meet immediately to work toward a major arms reduction, morality would be better served and many more people would join such a movement.

THE ERRORS AND EXTREME DANGER OF UTILITARIANISM

The great trouble with utilitarianism—which holds that we should maximize pleasure or happiness for the greater number of people— is that unlike religion and intuition, it doesn't even give us the PC. It lays the groundwork for wiping out one group of innocents after another so that those remaining can enjoy the greater pleasure: the old because they aren't producing anything; the young because there are too many of them; cripples because they are too much trouble; and this or that racial group because they are hated. It matters not that utilitarians say they don't want such mayhem, for its justification is in the very heart of the "greater pleasure for the greater number" principle; damned people are always interfering with the greater pleasure for the greater number.

Furthermore, utilitarianism is guilty of the naturalistic fallacy. Moore's question makes good sense to many of us: how do we know that pleasure should be our ultimate guide? (And how do we compare the years of pain of a researcher—or a political dissident, or a soldier in war—with the possible few moments of triumph?) Substituting "happiness" for "pleasure" only substitutes a vague word for a somewhat solid word, and leads nowhere that I can see, since to answer the question we would first need some specimens of people who call themselves happy, and I doubt we could find enough to conclude anything.

On secondary-code questions utilitarianism simply embarrasses itself, for it is all but impossible to apply the "greater pleasure" principle to such questions as homosexuality, divorce, capital punishment, gambling, alcohol, pornography, premarital sex, etc., and those utilitarians who give one answer are immediately confronted by other utilitarians with just the opposite answer.

It was a mistake to link the two codes; it was a worse mistake to bring in God to support the two codes; and it was an even worse mistake, when God began to fade for some, to move to the "greater pleasure" principle, which doesn't even give us the PC. From here Moore concluded that good is indefinable, and then the Logical Positivists capped it all off by arguing that "Stealing is wrong" means only that "I don't like stealing"—all of which would have led to total disaster were it not, fortunately, that the world had stopped paying attention to these philosophers, though we continued the dangerous linking of the two codes, even as we continued to lock up killers.

THE MYTH OF THE BASIC RIGHTS

The PC, not understood for what it is but essential to life, is always put in the popular language of the times—thus today we hear it said that people have a "fundamental right to live" and a "fundamental right not to be robbed and assaulted." Then, onto a good thing—who dares to deny these rights?—the moralist, the afflicted, the aggrieved, the offended, the annoyed, and the angry make anything important to them a "fundamental right"!

While it is certainly less than a precise way of explaining the nature of the PC, let's grant that people have a fundamental right to live, not to be assaulted, etc. (in other words, let's grant the PC as "rights"). The point then is that anything beyond the PC rights (free speech, freedom of assembly, and ramps for cripples in wheelchairs, for example) is the product of *opinion* on how political groups should conduct themselves or what services they should provide. If we call the PC proscriptions "fundamental rights," then they are the extent of fundamental rights, and anything else must be a secondary-code Right (the capital letter "R" indicating a special or metaphorical use of the word). A group cannot live without the PC rights, but perfectly legitimate groups (those that uphold the PC rights for all) have gotten along for centuries without any of the secondary-code Rights. But today the Rights have become mystified and it is a very risky business. It is easy enough to trace the source of the mystification.

Long before there were Rights, there were "wrongs" (e.g., it was wrong in England to criticize the Crown or to print anything without a license from the Crown) and the only way out, apparently, for those who would change the system (which included, of course, criticizing the Crown) was to declare right what had previously been called wrong. And the authority called upon to do this was the "Creator," "the laws of nature," and "self-evident truth," to quote from our own Declaration of Independence. Which is to say that the Rights were mystified and called moral from the beginning, and consequently, everyone else in the world who doesn't have these Rights is immoral. The phrases "Better dead than red" and "An empire of evil" are on the lips of the righteous, and every year the U.S. State Department issues a report card on the nations of the world, grading them according to our "morality," and we all arm ourselves, not knowing what will come next.

The extreme arrogance of the moralist and the danger he or she presents to everyone has seldom been more blatant than it is today, when the Western moralist, armed with his or her Rights, looks out at the world and condemns millions of others for their immorality. The claim is that these other people are enslaved by a handful of leaders, bureaucrats, and generals, but this is a fiction to hide the conviction that these millions are morally inferior, shown by the fact that, given the right circumstances, the Western moralist will bomb the hell out of them. I will never deny that there is just as much false morality on the other side, but since it is so easy for those in the West to see it, I need not go into it.

That these Rights are, in fact, political opinions concerning how a group should conduct itself and, thus, have nothing to do with morality can be glimpsed if we list some of them and what they lead to. In doing so perhaps we can appreciate why millions of people throughout the world are able to get along without them: the protection from self-incrimination (a defense for vicious killers and the like); free speech (the right to denounce God, country, and political leaders); freedom of the press (flooding a nation with pornography); the right to vote (illiterates and morons included); the right to bear arms (assassins picking up handguns at their local gun shops); freedom of assembly (including celebrations of hate); the right to form labor unions and to strike (the greater pain for the greater number); and the right to a public trial (where one's personal life may be exposed even though one is the victim, and where one receives a verdict from people with no training in the law).

If we drop the Creator and the laws of nature from the design, the Rights would seem to derive their sanction from two sources. First of all we like them very much—they are an addiction for those who have them and a passionate wanting for some people who do not have them.* Secondly, there is our conviction that these Rights restrain the powerful, and allow the system to adjust to wants, grievances, and injustices without constant revolution. Those who have the Rights are of the opinion that their society is safer, more just, and more enjoyable than it would be without them. However, if the Chinese had the Rights we do today, the question might arise whether they would eat tomorrow, which is an indication that the Rights, unlike the PC, are relative to time and circumstances. Hence, I end this section where I began: Rights are a matter of opinion as to how a group should conduct itself; to call them fundamental, basic, or moral makes millions of people immoral, and we already know what we have to do with the immoral.

SECONDARY CODES GONE MAD

The extreme result of linking secondary-code opinions with the PC

---

*How refreshing is Bertrand Russell's testimony of forty years ago: "I like democracy. I like individual liberty, and I like culture. I do not like to see ignorant or despotic officials interferring needlessly with private lives; I do not like to see creative thought crushed by the tyranny of stupid majorities. I do not like persecution, whether by majorities or minorities. I am suspicious of government and distrustful of politicians; but insofar as there must be government, I prefer it should be democratic," from "Citizenship in a Great State," *Fortune* (December, 1943). The reader is invited to shape his or her most deeply felt secondary-code beliefs into Russell's way of talking, where there is no mention of morality, or right or wrong.

truth is always death to someone—indeed, even millions of people. Let anything be tagged "moral," and let there be a lot of "immoral" people around, then sooner or later the solution has to be to wipe them out. Meanwhile, it is everyone's responsibility to harass them for their "immorality." Thus if homosexuality is considered immoral, there will not only be laws against the act,* but homosexuals may find themselves segregated and denied employment, a place to live, and even the basic protections of the PC—they may be abused, beaten, and killed with impunity. As the PC segregates and punishes the rapist and the murderer, so the secondary code may segregate and punish blacks, homosexuals, women, Catholics, Protestants, Jews, etc., listing so many wrongs they can commit (and that others can commit in their dealings with them) that they become different—what they say and even how they say it; where they walk and even how they walk; their very hopes and longings are subject to constant review, and if they protest they may be killed.

"Morality" tends to hide its responsibility in this sordid business, but let someone say—in certain societies or in certain places in this society—that there is nothing wrong with homosexuality, or marriage between the races,† or that a woman's place is not necessarily in the home, and "morality" will quickly uncover and reveal that it is, in fact, the ultimate authority for the laws, prejudices, and conventions that lock the subgroup in place. Morality—all that passes under this heading—is far too important

---

*I am not saying that a society cannot make sex between those of the same sex illegal and punish offenders. I am saying that the act is not immoral and that if it is banned (for whatever reason) then it is just like any other nonmoral law on the books: we can break it without being immoral, but we can also be punished without the group being immoral, provided the administration of the law is fair and just. I must say, however, that in the real world if homosexuality was not considered immoral, I doubt very much that it would be banned, for it is hard to think of a reason for banning it.

†At first glance it might seem that racial laws are not supported by "morality" but rather to preserve the white race. But if we probe further we invariably find that the reason the white race must be preserved is that whites are superior (including morally superior) to the other races, and, therefore, it would be immoral to "mix the races."

in most of our minds to allow us to get up in the morning with the only thought of what hateful, vicious thing we can do to our fellow human beings; hate, prejudice, punishment, and killing must have moral support or they die of shame.

Of even graver concern for these subgroups is that when things go wrong in a society the subgroups have been, on occasion, simply wiped out in the name of improving the society. With the secondary-code proscriptions tucked tightly in with the PC, it has not been easy for those in the subgroups to make a cogent argument; instead, they have been reduced to calling on God and other concepts equally vague. For example: "How does one determine whether a law is just or unjust? A just law squares with the moral law of God. An unjust law is out of harmony with the moral law of God."*

Only by severing the secondary code from morality can one say to another precisely what has to be said: "Your secondary code and all the rules, regulations, laws, conventions, and prejudices it supports in the name of morality are a day-in and day-out danger to me and my loved ones. You have created a reality more dangerous than any jungle. Your secondary code is immoral, and every day I obey its special laws against me, and am denied the laws that protect other members of society, is one day closer to the day when things will get even worse for me. Indeed, eventually you will destroy yourselves with this kind of thinking and behavior, for there is no limit to it. Disobeying these special laws is right, correct, and coherent, for how else can I awaken you to their wrongness if I don't tie up your police and courts that enforce them; the enforcement of which, up to now, I have administered by my compliance?" This is actually a restatement of a statement made by Dr. King† but without any of his religious arguments.

This sort of argument, in my opinion, is the moral foundation of civil disobedience: saying, in effect, that the PC comes first (even for the protesters in their struggle with the established order) but that the secondary code must be changed, for it is a threat to the

---

*Martin Luther King, Jr., *Why We Can't Wait* (New York: Signet, 1963), p. 82.

†Ibid., p. 76.

PC, and whatever threatens the PC is immoral. Needless to say, there are situations in which civil disobedience won't work. But now more than ever in this ever-shrinking world with ever-greater weaponry, morality demands compelling reasons for abandoning this option, and its warning is always the same: Allow idle killing and you are all going to die.

THE PROBLEM OF REDHEADS

Let me put the preceding argument more solidly within the framework of my basic argument. Institutionalized PC violations are immoral, although the time span here is glacial rather than immediate. A group will not long survive *one* killer or poisoner of the water supply or an arsonist freely going about his or her business, but a group can survive killing off or enslaving all of its redheads. But any enslavement or killing off of a subgroup must have a reason (e.g., racial inferiority, worshipping the wrong god, etc.), for without a reason there would be no way to explain that it was wrong for *one member of the dominant group to kill, assault, or enslave another member of the dominant group*, which is to say that the dominant group would not itself have the PC and it would quickly fall apart. Based on the historical evidence available, I would argue that dominant groups have always had their reasons and that if these reasons prevailed over a long period (and if there were not reforms), then the subgroup would eventually be wiped out and the same reasons would be used by survivors against other survivors until there was no one left. (I have referred before to a "French Revolution" of racial purity.) If we wiped out all the redheads because we didn't like them, then when all the redheads were gone, the reason (i.e., not liking people) would still stand and would be a reason for wiping out more people, and so on *ad infinitum*. And so, too, with racial purity and worshipping false gods; these are reasons given for enslaving, killing, and subjugating subgroups, and I think there is more than enough historical evidence available to justify the conclusion that unless there were reforms such thinking and behavior would lead to the destruction of everything. Up to now, often after a lot of bloodshed, there usually have been reforms before groups have totally wiped themselves out; but as long as any people have their reasons for subjugating and killing subgroups (or other groups for that matter), then this error in thinking (given the desire that everything not be destroyed) threatens to become infectious and, in time, we will all die. In short, racial subjugation or religious intolerance is an extremely risky business and is immoral, although the time span here is, as I have said, glacial rather than immediate. (Although, looking at the world as of this moment, it would seem that we are in a race against time.)

"REVERENCE FOR LIFE"

It has not been my intention to restrict the reader or anyone else from proposing a new criterion broader than that which gives us the PC (in other words, a guide broader than the ultimate and all-but-universal desire that everything not be destroyed) and urging the world to hold this desire as well, and therefore proscribe all those acts not in keeping with its satisfaction. What I am advocating is that for everyone's safety, those with a broader desire or criterion in mind recognize what they are really doing and stop beating the world over the head—as they have so often done in the past—with the charge of immorality, when the world is guilty of nothing more than not sharing a broader criterion. With this in mind, let me turn to one final theory of morality.

Some people hold to a criterion far broader than that which gives us the PC, namely, *that all life be preserved whenever possible.* This criterion leads to a specific position on abortion, capital punishment, vivisection, and meat-and fish-eating. But it is one thing to propose this criteron (and be personally guided by it) and quite another to call these acts, in violation of such a position, immoral. For the latter really says no more than that what guides me should guide you, but since it does not and since I have been unable to convince you that it should, I will instead call you bad names, i.e., immoral. Millions of human beings, living strictly within the bounds of the PC and wanting no innocent human being harmed, do want to eat meat and fish; do want murderers killed; and do favor abortion and vivisection for the simple reason that they are not guided by the criterion that all life be preserved whenever possible. That's reality; that's the way things are; and if you want to change the way things are, then face the fact that you must greatly expand the basic criterion, and that nothing is gained but a lot is risked by calling half the world immoral. (The Australian philosopher Peter Singer has asked me, "What responsibility do we have toward those who can't speak for themselves, e.g., human fetuses?" My basic answer is that the innocent are inviolable, and we dare not kill any of them or stand by while any of them are being killed without at the same time threatening the destruction of everything. But this answer does not give clear direction on the question of abortion, for the facts here seem to be that to forbid abortion does not stop it, and women die in the process of having illegal abortions. We are thus faced with a tortured matter of opinion.)

When morality is reduced to what you and your side want, needless to say, the door is open to an extremely dangerous relativism, for who is to say no to anyone who feels moral? Those who try to pass "reverence for life" off as morality are reinforcing the most dangerous fanatic's belief that morality is what he or she believes it to be. There is no reason for me to be coy: I am as frightened of the "reverence for life" school as I am of any moralist, for certainly if one of them is put in charge of things it will be open season on hunters, fish- and meat-eaters, and pregnant women who have anything less than an ecstatic look on their faces.

Abortion, euthanasia, vivisection, and capital punishment are tortured questions for many of us for the *very reason* that they are *not* moral (the ultimate guide doesn't guide) and there are elements in our own minds that will be deeply offended however we decide them.

You pull the switch on a murderer or you tell the victim's family the killer will be out in five years; *you* cut open a cat or you tell the suffering that medical research must be delayed; *you* dispose of a fetus or you tell a woman in torment that she must go to full term; *you* let a man in excruciating pain go on for another month or so, or you allow the old to live in terror that every time they catch a cold some petty functionary will decide it is time for them to go. Do this, or else admit that the other person has his or her opinion, just as you have yours, and that morality is no help at all, even though life is involved and a terrible decision has to be made.

MORALITY'S ATTIC

In morality's attic there are a lot of odd, rare, ridiculous, and interesting questions that no more affect the structure of morality than anything stored in an attic ordinarily affects a house or the people living in it. But let us take a look at some of these questions just to make sure:

• One reason moral philosophers have had such a terrible time figuring out the nature of morality is that they often started with nonmoral questions, and highly artificial ones at that (questions that were, instead, tortured matters of opinion). One of the most famous examples—and one that is still used in ethics classes— was posed by the English philosopher William Godwin (1756-1836), who asked the reader whom he would save from a burning building if he or she could save only one—a valet who happened to be the reader's father, or a world-renowned writer.* The answer is that there is no one answer, and that is the very reason people have found the question interesting and why it has persisted; when the lives of two innocents are at stake and one must die, morality is silent. Generally speaking, morality is a very dull business, as dull as a jail cell; opinion is interesting, but opinion passing as *the* moral answer is too interesting.

• The story goes that when Gertrude Stein was asked what she would do if by pulling a switch she could save her brother from certain death but would kill five hundred Chinese instantly, she was so upset by the question that she went to bed for a week. Here morality has a firm answer: You always save the greater number of innocents, since any other approach or consideration could lead to the destruction of everything, which becomes clear if we expand

---

*William Godwin, *Enquiry Concerning Human Justice* (Oxford, England: Clarendon Press; 1971), p. 71.

the five hundred Chinese to everyone in the world except Ms. Stein and her brother. The reason this answer may not be clearly understood is that such situations seldom arise in real life, but if they did it would be obvious that we would have to make it policy always to go for the fewer deaths, and punish Ms. Stein if she chose to save her brother. Indeed, if such dilemmas were common, society would have to pass a law requiring us to sacrifice our own lives, and kill us if we didn't. But since this situation is very rare, no laws have been needed, and the word "coward" has served as punishment enough, with those saying the word often not at all sure what they would do in a similar situation.

• Just as there are "sins of omission" in religion, so there are "wrongs of omission" in morality, but they are so rare that for the most part they have not been incorporated into our laws, which is by way of saying that something can be immoral but not illegal. If Mr. Johnson can save little Susan by throwing her a life preserver, then it would be immoral not to, which would be clear if the situation were common; a group is simply not going to survive if people ignore cries for help. While it would be incorrect to punish Johnson for failing to save Susan, since there is no law on the books against his immorality, condemnation is definitely called for.

• Saving lives often guides public policy, but taken to extremes, labeling as morality anything that saves lives can be very dangerous policy, for it confuses the true nature of morality, which is not saving lives at any cost, but rather keeping the group and life going. When a firehouse is closed for budgetary reasons, the cry that people will die is often heard along with the charge that the budget-slashers are immoral. This charge is untrue and a corruption of morality, for short of a firehouse on every block and massive interference in people's lives, some are going to die in fires. And morality is silent on the number, which is why the question is so difficult. (Yes, given enormous numbers of people dying in fires, firehouses can be a moral question.) The "savers of lives" are an extremely arrogant lot going on the assumption, as they do, that they are doing "good"; they are not doing good, and while they are not doing evil either (beyond confusing the nature of morality), if they are left to have their way, we will all live under a fascism of safety.

• Incest is, as it were, the duckbill platypus of morality, not the only odd beast in the zoo, but one of the oddest in that it is hard to know in which category it belongs. Some acts of incest are nothing less than assaults on the innocent, and are immoral for that reason, but other acts of incest (say, between "consenting" siblings) are not so clearly wrong. There is also, however, genetic evidence against incest, which over a long period might lead to the destruction of the group. Finally, there is now all-but-universal opinion against *any* incest. So incest is an interesting question, but not, I believe, threatening to my main argument (just as the platypus is interesting but not ultimately threatening to the theory behind the classification of animals), particularly since genetics and opinion are both lined up against it and there is no serious debate over allowing it.

• Hundreds of questions beyond the ones I have been concentrating on are or have been called moral or ethical by some people. Let a student get caught smoking pot, and he or she may be hauled before the "Students' Ethics Committee"; let two principles come into conflict in medicine, law, business, or government, and it is immediately assumed that we are faced with a "moral dilemma"; let a "vigorous game player" push the rules a bit far, and the losers often cry immorality. Mostly these questions have nothing to do with morality, and nothing is gained by calling them moral—all we get is needless confusion and anger, since compromise is then impossible without a deep sense of "betraying one's principles." Recognize these questions as matters of opinion and one can relax—the jails are always there to receive the immoral and those who break the non-PC laws, and morality is not threatened either by "sacrificing your principles" or by the other fellow's winning the day. My own belief—at least my own hope—is that as we come to see the splendor of morality for what it is, we will also recognize the true sacrilege of calling anything else moral.

THE YOUNG

If there is any hope of unlinking the two codes, it will be, I believe, in what we teach the young. Specifically, we must narrow the use of the words "morality," "immorality," "right," "wrong," "good," and "bad" and thereby limit what passes for morality, and either put all other matters into the political arena or let them be "free choices" (which is not to say that we cannot offer guidance on the "free choices" and the risks they may involve). We must correct our children's use of the words "moral," "immoral," etc., when these words are used incorrectly, and teach them why, despite appearances, "Murder is wrong" and "Abortion is wrong" are two substantively different statements.* The young soon understand that they cannot have everything that they want and they come to understand that they cannot compromise with morality. However, if too much of what they want is placed under the heading of morality, then we have taken the world of wanting and put it into the world of "must have," and that is disaster. We must teach them differently.

The possibilities are intriguing—for the young would no longer feel immoral if they compromised their secondary-code judgments, or even if they accepted defeat, while any use of the heavy linguistic artillery of the PC to push one's opinion would cause embarrassment and laughter—the audience laughing at the speaker's misuse of language and the speaker embarrassed at being laughed at.

I am not optimistic that such an approach will ever be adopted, for it entails the problem I have discussed before of acknowledging that we are in the area of opinion on matters that are very important to us. If someone feels his or her position is

---

*My greatest triumph in life came in a bar one night, or early morning, when a friend with whom I had been arguing the question of abortion finally cried out, "OK, OK, so *it is* a matter of opinion, *so what—my* opinion is an emphatic *no* to abortion!" Never again did I hear my friend argue the question of abortion beyond saying he was against it. He was changed in heart and in mind by uttering the word "opinion." It was all over; he was ready for a show of hands, and be done with it.

right, linguistic analysis is probably not going to make much of a dent; there will be tremendous psychological resistance on everyone's part to admitting that some beliefs have nothing to do with morality. Most of us looking out at the world can clearly see the enormous amount of political opinion and religious beliefs masquerading as truth and morality—and the bloody results. But when the matter is of great importance to us, we, too, only see truth and right. Most of us have at least one opinion that we believe is truth and that would drive us to bloodshed—and, not surprisingly, there is, therefore, a lot of bloodshed in the world: a bloody mix of religion, politics, nationalism, and fear, but moral righteousness is always in support of the actual killing, for when it comes to killing anyone or supporting such policies most of us simply can't do it unless we believe we are right and the other side is wrong. One hundred million killed in this century alone, and all of them killed in the name of "right." (Yet we ponder heavily the "moral" questions of capital punishment, abortion, and vivisection; it would make a Martian laugh or cry at the order of our concerns.)

How much passion could a leader stir if he or she were forced by convention to begin a speech, "In my opinion . . ."? And how many young men and women would go off to battle under the banner "We are very annoyed!"? Generally speaking, the more moral the rhetoric, the further we are from morality. In World War II the young accepted the draft, and those who were rejected often lied and cheated to get into the armed services, while in the Vietnam War the young screamed, lied, and cheated to stay out; one war was a clear threat to all life, since we had no idea of the limits the other side would go to if it won, while the other was not, and the young sensed the difference. They still sense the difference, but they must have words to express it and a standard against which to correct their leaders.

At lectures on world affairs a hand inevitably goes up and a voice asks, "But what can I do?" Whatever the failings of my lecture, here at least I have an answer: "You can place the word 'opinion' in front of all your serious thoughts, and when speaking what is on your mind, take out the word 'opinion' only if it would cause your statement to sound ridiculous. Teach your children to do the same. And laugh at those who don't."

Afterword

There was a time when Random House had accepted this book and was preparing it for publication; indeed, the galleys had already been printed. For reasons I shall explain momentarily, Random House dropped the book, but before it was removed from their publication list, Jason Epstein, my editor at Random House, asked me to write an Afterword. What follows is the Afterword more or less as I prepared it for him. Needless to say, I am deeply endebted to Prometheus Books and to Paul Kurtz, its president and editor in chief, for bringing this project to its completion; and to Steven L. Mitchell, my editor, who supervised the production of this volume in its present form. Some of the others to whom I am endebted have already been mentioned in the Acknowledgments and still others will be found in this Afterword.

The publication of this book has had, to say the least, an unusual history, a history that has raised serious doubts in the minds of more than a few people about my qualifications for saying anything at all about morality. Therefore I want to say a word or two about what happened and, more important, to relate it to the arguments of this book. But before doing this, let me say who I am and how my ideas came to be—for that is all relevant to the incident I want to discuss.

I am not a professional philosopher, but I have always been a

147

philosopher. When I was a child I asked a question—long since forgotten—that elicited the contemptuous reply from my teacher, "What do we have here, a little philosopher?" If I could have a dollar for every time someone has said to me with the same contempt, "What are you, a philosopher?" or "You think too much," I would be rich. Philosophical questions have their place, but when people are trying to do their work, such questions can be extremely annoying.

Early in my career, in addition to wanting to be a philosopher, I wanted to be a king, but I soon settled for being a press secretary to kings and would-be kings, or more precisely, for working in press relations for a number of people in local and state government, and for any number of candidates for public office. I cannot imagine any better training for a philosopher of morality. I came to admire the American politician and his or her instinctive understanding that most questions are not moral but political, even as, in my own way, I urged politicians to be a trifle bolder in expressing this belief.

I was born in Milwaukee, Wisconsin, in 1929, but grew up in Manhattan, where I have spent most of my life. I went to Ethical Culture School and later to Trinity School. Religion has always been a part of my life. I was baptized a Catholic, confirmed in the Episcopal Church, and, after instruction, married in the Catholic Church. I still pray every day, enter churches to pray and meditate, and believe in God and an afterlife. I am also convinced, however, that religion has no role to play in our understanding of right and wrong. As I indicated earlier in the book, I find the argument that accuses theologians and prophets of committing a fallacy to be devastating. Religion is to get us through dark nights; it is not for instruction on how to behave.

Because of my great difficulty with learning foreign languages, I was in chronic trouble in college; indeed, I went to three of them, ending up finally with a B.A. from Columbia College, which had excused me from the language requirement. At Columbia I took a course in ethics and was left traumatized by the dreadful conclusion that rational men and women could not agree on what morality was, leaving the door open to a frightful relativism. This problem has troubled me ever since, and the study of morality was the one area where I continued my (informal) education.

Racial discrimination also had a profound effect on my early years, although before I ran across it, I had not even thought of the race question. I first experienced it while serving as a paratrooper at Fort Campbell, Kentucky, in 1953. As long as I live, I will never forget the first time my train entered the land of Jim Crow and a conductor, looking to me like a madman, ran through my car crying, "Nigras only, nigras only." I was horrified and could think of nothing else for weeks. Out of the Army and with Jim Crow still smoldering in my brain, I joined the staff of the New York City Commission on Human Rights as assistant press secretary. From there I went to the New York City Department of Labor as press secretary, and later to the mayor's office, where I was assistant press secretary to Mayor Robert F. Wagner. And all this time—the fifties and early sixties—I was involved with one political candidate or another.

During the fifties I wrote a book called *Ultimate Desires*, which as far as I know was the first book in philosophy ever to consider desire as a significant element in our understanding of language and truth. But when I tried to get it published, I came up against what has been the Catch-22 of my life: trade publishers—that is, publishers of general, nonacademic books—had little or no interest in formal philosophy, and I had no credentials to satisfy the demands of a university press. I had difficulty even getting a reading; finally, in 1958, I paid to have my book published. This book needed a lot of editing (which it did not get), but still I am proud of it and feel—even now that there is more interest in the concept of desire among philosophers—it was far in advance of its time.

In 1965, I became executive secretary of the New York City Council Against Poverty. When John Lindsay became mayor, he appointed me director of civil defense and assigned me to abolish the office. The idea of abolishing one's own office was new at the time and created quite a stir in the media, and for a few brief moments I was a celebrity. The *New York Times* called me "Man in the News," with the slug under my name reading "Philosophical Paratrooper"—it was my finest moment. I completed my task without trouble, and Mayor Lindsay then appointed me assistant administrator of the Housing and Development Administration. Despite the vast size of this bureaucracy, little housing or development was being done, and in 1968 I quit city government to do press relations and fund-raising for Harlem Fight Back, a self-supporting civil-rights organization run by James Haughton that seeks to get blacks and Puerto Ricans jobs in the construction trades. I lasted three years. Working in Harlem put me in a deep depression, which was not helped by the fact that I had begun to drink heavily. My last paid job, in 1971, was as a one-year consultant to Prime Minister Lynden O. Pindling of the Bahamas as that country prepared for independence.

The drinking got worse until finally I made a compromise with it. I turned to Antabuse—a drug that makes one sick if one drinks—and stayed on it for three to six months at a time, then took "mini-vacations" of between five and ten days, when I did nothing but drink.

In the seventies the "me generation" replaced the war protesters and civil-rights demonstrators. I wrote a book satirizing such egocentric views as Ayn Rand's and called it *The Ego and the Machine*. In trying to get it published, I ran across another variation of Catch-22—it is hard to get a publisher's reading without an agent, but it is equally hard to attract an agent without some published writings. With some money left over from the sale of a house, I published *The Ego* under the pseudonym T. R. Cullen.

The Ego failed badly as satire. I enclosed a reply card in each book, and of the 270 I got back, only one even mentioned the word "satire." Many readers loved it—"The best thing since Ayn Rand," one said—and many hated it. I soon abandoned promoting it, since some obviously were using it as a how-to-get-ahead-in-life book. However, in the process of writing it I stumbled across something that would ultimately become the germ of my theory that two different things pass for morality. In *The Ego* I dismissed morality altogether, but what I was really doing was dismissing secondary code "morality," and this was *not* satire (secondary codes passing as morality ought to be dismissed as morality, if we are to survive) even though I did not appreciate what I was doing at the time. In other words, I was on my way to several of the arguments of this current book.

In real life—life outside my satire—I was sure I could not dismiss all of morality, but if there was part of it that should be dismissed, then there would be a division—the question was along what lines. I wrote a paper titled "What Is Morality?" in which I argued that what passes for morality is actually divisible into two substantively different matters. I referred to "universal shockers" (those acts that shock everyone; the acts I mentioned were not far from what I now call the PC acts) and "half-world shockers" (the ones I listed were the same ones I now list under secondary-code questions). For example, murder and arson are "universal shockers," while abortion and homosexuality are "half-world shockers." I sent this paper to dozens of philosophers and a half dozen journals but received only one reply, from Peter Singer, the Australian philosopher, who crushed me and my paper with the charge that I was guilty of committing the naturalistic fallacy. As he wrote, "Just because an act shocks everyone doesn't prove to me that it is necessarily wrong." The naturalistic fallacy! That slayer of a thousand theories of morality.

I sent a quick thank-you note to Singer and said that a long letter would follow. I then went into what can only be described as a period of frenzied thinking, determined to say what morality is and to escape the problem of the naturalistic fallacy. I walked the streets of Manhattan day and night, often for three days on end, unable to stop thinking. I was grateful I lived where I did, since in Manhattan no one pays any attention to someone dressed without care and talking audibly to himself or herself, and supplying audible answers, too. (It was during this period that I came to put the word "opinion" in front of all my precious beliefs and took it out only when it made the sentence sound truly ridiculous—e.g., "In *my opinion* murder is wrong"—and I became a very changed person for having done this, namely, I lost a lot of my passion for my secondary-code opinions.) The experience was all but psychedelic, and went on for about three months. Then, fearing for my well-being, I drank for a week to shut down my brain for a time. Sobering up, I started throwing words on paper, and at the end of three years I had my answer for Singer and what was, in fact, the first draft of this book. I sent it off to him. His reply was long, detailed, and technical but included this statement: "I would not say that you have here deduced morals from fact, but what you have shown is that given certain desires which all of us have, it follows that accepting certain values will be the only way to fulfill our desires. I think you are justified in claiming that this [my argument] gets around a substantial part of the problem of the Naturalistic Fallacy, and shows that one can have morality that is in some sense objective for all human beings, without committing the Naturalistic Fallacy." I nearly fainted! If Singer was correct, I had done what no one else had done before, and the fact that no one else was even bothering to try anymore, heightened, not lessened, my excitement.

But now my troubles began. Whatever the realities of my situation and those of the publishing industry and academia, here is what I perceived:

• The fortress that is the publishing industry had not weakened during the twenty-five years since I had tried to get a reading for *Ultimate Desires*.

• Among the few literary agents who replied to the many inquiries I sent out along with the Singer letter and the introduction to my book, the verdict was unanimous and borderline contemptuous of my chances. One agent wrote that philosophy and morality are among the most difficult genres for which to find a national trade publisher, particularly for an author who does not have a "track record" or academic credentials, and he warned that most agents are unable to take on a manuscript that is so hard to sell, no matter what they may think of it. Still another variation of Catch-22.

• I sent the manuscript, along with the Singer letter, to the heads of fifty philosophy departments in the hope of winning some "credentials" in academia, namely, letters of support and praise for my discoveries about morality and the nature of language, but I did not receive any replies, beyond a few acknowledgments that the material had been received.

• I became increasingly aware that the manuscript was in need of serious structural revision and that it was full of redundancies, but without editorial help I was not confident of how to revise it.

• Then someone said something that alarmed me—"You are sending the manuscript to too many people; your central ideas about language and morality are clearly stated and easily stolen."

The story now unfolds along two parallel courses—one having to do with my efforts to get a reading in the publishing industry at large, and the other, my attempt to get a particular publisher, Jason Epstein, editorial director of Random House, to read it. Both parts of the story occurred during November and December 1983. Let me start with the industry at large:

Increasingly worried that I was not even going to get a reading without an agent, having been unable to get one, and fearing that my ideas might be appropriated by others, I took an extremely long but calculated gamble. If philosophy departments would not give me the "credentials" I needed—letters of praise for my discoveries—I would bestow them on myself. I went to a printer and had a memo pad made up with the name of one of America's foremost philosophers on it. I then wrote a glowing tribute to my book on a sheet from this pad and signed the philosopher's name. I told no one that this letter was a forgery and began by showing it to a few friends, who accepted it eagerly at face value. Whether I formally submitted this "letter" with the Singer letter and a copy of the introduction to publishers, I am not certain, but I think I did, though I have no replies in my file. In any case, I did send the letter to at least a half dozen people whom I had at one time or another run across and who were in or around the publishing industry—writers, copy editors, and magazine people. And I was aware that at least one of them made copies of the forgery and sent them to people who might help me.

I knew that as fulsome as the forged letter was, no publisher would publish my book simply because of the letter, but that was not what I was after—I was after a reading. I also knew that my forgery would eventually be exposed—at least if the book was accepted—but my hope was that my book would be in print before this happened and that it might find a life of its own, independent of its author. I planned to concentrate on trade publishers, partly because I believed they would be less suspicious of such a letter than the university presses, and partly because I believed that once my book was read, its importance would be clear enough that its appeal to general readers would also be recognized, and therefore it would not be treated by reviewers as "just another university press book." Indeed, some excitement might be generated by the very fact that a trade publisher was doing a book on philosophy, since even the famous philosopher whose name I had forged was published by a university press.

Now to Random House where things were complex. What I thought to be true and what was actually true may be quite different, but let me say what I thought to be true. At Random House I was not unknown. My problem was that I was known all too well. Years earlier, when I had been drinking heavily, I had known Jason Epstein socially, and I simply had to believe that he did not think much of me. I, on the other hand, came to be aware of him as a quite special editor, in that if an author had an idea Epstein felt was worthwhile he was willing to work considerably harder than most editors at formulating it into a book. And I was aware I needed this for my book, for I knew I had not presented my ideas as well as I might have.

With this background I was quite certain that the chances were slim that Epstein would have the slightest interest in even looking at a book by me; yet, I had no choice but long shots anyway. In mid-November 1983, I sent him the introduction and the Singer letter (but not the forged letter). Within a few weeks I received a letter from Epstein saying in part, "This kind of writing doesn't usually interest me but the few pages that you've sent seem sensible and lively. . . . I would like to read the manuscript itself."

But there was also some bad luck. While Epstein hadn't seen the forged letter, he had heard about it from a mutual friend of ours and when the friend called to congratulate me on my progress, she told me that Epstein also wanted to see the letter, and that I should send it along with the manuscript, which I did. A week later Epstein accepted the book. How much the letter weighed in Epstein's deliberations is impossible for me to measure, and I can only pass on what Epstein subsequently said to me: "Many factors go into a decision on a manuscript such as yours, but it was the manuscript itself and not the letter that convinced me to proceed. The letter by itself meant nothing."

A question I can better answer is why I didn't admit to Epstein, once he offered me a contract, that the letter was a forgery. Here was my thinking at the time, as nearly as I can remember it: I put myself in the shoes of any editor of a major house—accepting a book on morality by an admitted forger might be tolerable, but that the forgery could be associated with the very acceptance of the book would be intolerable for an editor to bear and might make him or her a laughingstock (so I thought). Another reason for not admitting the forgery is that, because I had already circulated the letter, I was certain to be found out whether or not I admitted the forgery and was, therefore, in deep trouble in any case; the question for me was whether to be in deep trouble with a book or in deep trouble without a book, for even if Epstein were to cancel the book and not reveal his real reasons, the facts would probably come out and I would be dead in the water. Furthermore, I had no reason to assume that Epstein would conceal his real reasons, for he certainly owed his fellow editors more than he did a forger. In any case, I did not tell Epstein and prayed that I would have a book before I was found out, for I was certain that my discoveries about the nature of language were of lasting value. Even if the book was ignored for ten years because of the world's annoyance with me, it would, in time, emerge on its own.

Epstein and I began editing the book, but it soon became apparent to him that the job would require more time than he could devote to it. Consequently, Epstein retained Jonathan Lieberson as a consultant. He and I worked for hundreds of hours making my arguments into a more orderly and sharper book, and showing our work to Epstein for criticism or approval. The manuscript was not ready for the typesetter until September 1984, ten months after the contract was signed, but while being set, the deception was discovered. I had always been prepared for this moment, and I called the philosopher whose name I had used and said, among other things: "I am sorry, but I did what I believed I had to do to get my book read. That the letter turned out not to be needed for a reading was an ironic and unexpected twist of my fate."

On September 13, the story broke in the *New York Times*. Epstein told the newspaper that he was undecided as to what to do, but that the had asked me to explain fully why I did what I did and how it fit into my argument about the nature of morality, and depending on this explanation he would decide whether or not to publish. (I believe, but am by no means certain, that Epstein wanted to publish right up to the end, but that he was overruled by those in higher authority at Random House. In any case, I was informed in mid-November of the decision not to publish.) I have explained the why of what I did; now let me relate it to my analysis of morality.

Many people assumed that what I did was immoral because it involved a lie, but lying is not necessarily immoral and, indeed, in certain situations it can be the moral thing to do, e.g., telling an axe murderer the axe is in the basement when in fact it is in the attic. Nevertheless, what I did was immoral—it was an act of stealing and if I was free to keep at it, and not restricted by tighter security in other fields, there is no limit to the destruction I could cause as I forged the names of political leaders and army commanders. Forgery, in other words, is one of those acts that has to be curbed, condemned, and punished, since its potential for disaster is too dangerous to make subtle distinctions as to the field one is in and the motivations of the forgerer.

It is important to keep in mind, however, that when we say an act is morally wrong, we are not putting the burden on the individual not to do it; the burden is on the group not to permit it and to punish those who do it. (This must always be the real burden on the would-be violator—punishment, and what he or she agrees to or doesn't agree to, or what he or she thinks, is not important.) In my case the most obvious punishment is not to publish the book, which would have the further effect of deterring others. Nevertheless, there is a unique and interesting problem here—the book and I, while intimately related, are two different things and the group does not want to be in the position of automatically rejecting all books as a way of punishing authors who have done something truly wrong in trying to get their books published. Furthermore, I have not gone unpunished: I have been widely condemned for what I did; my stature as a would-be philosopher has been permanently stunted (I had no stature to be reduced); and I am sure that a lot of people I was trying to reach will now ignore the book because of the forgery. Indeed, one professor at a major university has recommended to the American Philosophical Association that it support a boycott of my book. While this seems to me a silly if not an impossible form of punishment, it does reflect the degree of anger in academia. The question, then, is the form and degree of punishment; my point is that I have not gone unpunished.

Contrary to the recommendation that my book be boycotted, another distinguished professor of philosophy, now retired, wrote a letter to Lieberson following press reports of the forgery, saying that in his view the decision whether to publish had to be based strictly on the book's merits, the exposure of the author as a forger notwithstanding. Jason Epstein, in an initial reaction to the question of publishing, said that he would never consider hiring me as an accountant for Random House but would consider publishing the book based on its merits if I gave an account of my actions that fit the facts of the case as he knew them—hence this Afterword.

At the other end of the spectrum (in opposition to those who don't want the book published) are those who slap me on the back and say, "Right on!" and "Sock it to 'em!" as if I were a modern version of Robin Hood. This is very embarrassing to me and totally contrary to my position on morality. Robin Hood was wrong because stealing is wrong. Except in extreme circumstances the morally correct way to change an intractable political system is by civil disobedience, with the possible addition of nonlethal sabotage. Indeed, a president of an eastern college, who got in on the debate over my forgery, said that what I should have done was camp outside of a publisher's office until I got my reading—and I think he is very right, it is what I should have done.

Another question involves the betrayal or at least the embarrassment of people who trusted me. Here I can only appeal to what I felt was my desperate situation and say that I am sorry for the trouble I caused others, just as a starving man can say to the person he stole the money from that he is sorry, but he really felt he had no choice—except to die (or, in my case, to go unread and unpublished). I did not forge the letter so that my book would be published, I forged it to get a reading; but once my book was read (and, ironically, accepted by someone who had asked to see the manuscript before hearing about the letter), it was my opinion that I could not reveal the forgery without causing the whole project to crumble. But all the reasons in the world cannot excuse that act; I only hope that the damage to the book is not too great.

At Home On

St. Simons

Eugenia Price

PEACHTREE PUBLISHERS LIMITED

Published by
PEACHTREE PUBLISHERS, LTD.
494 Armour Circle, N. E.
Atlanta, Georgia 30324

Copyright © 1981   Eugenia Price, Text
Critt Graham, Illustrations

Manufactured in the United States of America

Book and cover design by Critt Graham

First Edition

ISBN: 0-931948-16-9
Library of Congress Catalog Card Number 81-1412

For Carol and the late Larry Case, who first published these columns, and for my mother, who bothered to save them.

Contents

To Be Read First

I am writing these lines at the beginning of a new decade—
the decade of the 1980s—after having lived almost twenty
years on St. Simons Island, Georgia. They are certainly not
the first lines I've written about the lush, sheltering, buggy,
enchanted cosmos that is this particular coastal island. Over
the past years there have been three novels laid here, plus *St.
Simons Memoir* and *Diary of a Novel*. In all these, as
historical fiction and autobiography, I have attempted to
delineate the essence of this once wild little island cosmos.

My dictionary declares that "cosmos" means "the universe
conceived as an orderly, harmonious system." St. Simons a
universe? Orderly? Harmonious? Its nature, yes. Season
follows season in nature's orderly fashion. Cardinals mate
with other cardinals; azalea bushes sprout azalea buds,
wisteria vines wisteria buds; French mulberries and star-
flowers appear on schedule. Still, where people live, they
intervene to change natural order and harmony; and people
have been *busy* on my island. "Order" seems to be missing
entirely from our development, and at least the old "harmony" among islanders has lessened. It is no longer safe to leave
doors unlocked or to walk alone on the beach. "Harmonious" certainly does not describe the performance of the local
government. More trees are falling, the woods are being
hacked and bulldozed away. And yet I stick with that word
"cosmos."

Distinct from the other barrier islands off the coast of
Georgia, St. Simons is, in its own way, a small, unique
universe, harmonious and orderly at its core—its soul—in
spite of external disorder and rampant growth; different, in a
way no one has yet managed to explain. And perhaps this

1

very difference springs from the fact that its history *is* singular. You see, unlike the other islands, St. Simons has never been privately owned. That is, except for God, who thought it up in the first place, no one owner has ever legally been in possession of St. Simons Island. In a sense, I suppose one could say that the colonial government of Georgia owned it back in the 1700s, but even then its population was as varied and individual as now. No one family has ever cared for, planted, or guarded it. Even in his day, the Spaniards gave General Oglethorpe a hard time protecting it. Then at a later period, roughly twelve plantation families owned the little strip of land.

And now look! I am told that more than twelve hundred houses will be built soon in the vicinity of Christ Church on the as yet unspoiled end of the island at Frederica, close by the fort. There aren't enough of us in this section now to get cable TV. How much change will twelve hundred new buildings cause? How much disorder? How much disharmony?

Perhaps not too much, really. And my ability to write that proves to me, at least, that the *un*changing, harmonious, orderly cosmic heart of this island has at last penetrated *me*. Once the mere thought of the destruction of these "dear, dark woods" made me physically ill. Oh, the beauty as we all know it now, around Christ Church and Fort Frederica, will be drastically changed. Frederica will look much like any other subdivision. There is talk of St. Simons being incorporated so that we will no longer be a helpless, rather affluent appendage of the sprawling Glynn County government. On the other hand, there is talk of consolidation with the remainder of the county, which, of course, would make us an instant city—I presume called Brunswick. Change and the threats of change buffet us daily.

2

But can such radical changes really wipe out the *inner* essence of the unique little cosmos that for years has attracted even United States presidents in need of shelter and peace and rest and a restored sense of wonder?

When Joyce Blackburn and I first discovered this light-struck, tree-and-vine-choked small cosmos back in 1961, St. Simons was simple and quiet and lovely and slow—affluent only in its singular beauty. Islanders were mainly warm-hearted, easy-living folk. *Less* than 3,000 strong. Each a strong individualist, in his or her own way; each an Islander. I see us beginning to blur together now. There are four times as many Islanders, and our "master plan" anticipates 20,000 more!

Do I deplore this? Yes, for obvious reasons. And yet I don't altogether deplore it, because each new person who makes the final drive across the marshes and salt creeks to live on St. Simons "forever," as we did, seems as much in love with it and as full of joy to be here as were we all those years ago. For these growing numbers of newcomers, the old magic holds. The cosmos remains. They are *on* St. Simons—at last—to stay. I confess at times to marveling at their joy and gladness, because the Island is so changed for me. And yet, and yet, even the ongoing debate about a second causeway and the four-laning of Frederica and Demere roads in no way seems to dim the newcomer's elevation of spirit at having "come home" at last.

"Four-lane Frederica Road?" a new resident gasped when I mentioned it to her in the grocery store the other day. Her face pale, she reeled a little, and then that determined smile returned, as her color returned. "Well, it's still St. Simons Island, and I don't want to be any other place on the face of this old earth!"

Nor do I.

Of course a new causeway, or four-laning the present one over a ghastly, high, view-distorting set of bridges, is supposed to make it safe for Islanders when hurricanes and tidal waves come. Well, I no longer fear the Island's geography, and, except for moments of stabbing memory, I have stopped being afraid for St. Simons. I loathe what is happening; but you see, some mystical part of the Island's core has entered mine. For a time, I considered calling this book *Inner Island*. Living here for twenty years has helped me find an inner island of my own. A quiet, inner refuge where, some of the time at least, God and I attempt to keep me grateful and accepting. I have stopped fighting. Today, from my office window, I can still see only live oaks and breeze-stirred moss and pine trees and lush sweet gum leaves. If I walk to my bedroom window, I can still see the small back marsh, where spider webs go on glistening at dawn and out of which a full moon continues to rise.

Servicemen still come promptly when appliances break down, and the people at Georgia Power and Southern Bell are still kind and sympathetic when we call to report trouble. Our storekeeper friends seldom lose their smiles when my readers go on trying to find out where I live; and Sarah Edmond and Monroe Wilson are friends and not just employees who come to clean our house and mow our lawn. A meal at Alphonza Ramsey's Plantation Club, at Blanche's Courtyard, or at Gantt's is as warm and welcoming an experience as a meal on Lorah Plemmons's back porch once was. This may all change when those terrifying population projections are at last fact. But I choose to believe not.

My period of rebellion at what "they're doing" to St. Simons seems, at least most of the time, to have passed. The

4

heart of the once wild, nearly primitive little cosmos remains: the enduring essence, which I pray has really become a part of me.

Day follows day and St. Simons goes on, unprotected by single ownership or even by state or federal ownership as with the other barrier islands. Perhaps it garners inner strength from this very fate of having fallen into the hands of lots and lots of people, some of whom still seem intent upon grabbing more and more money from it for themselves.

I've been accused of that, and I understand the accusation. God knows that when I wrote *The Beloved Invader,* my first novel laid here, I had no earthly reason to believe that it would sell as it did and bring people flocking to Christ Church at Frederica, books in hand, to search out the graves of my main characters who lie buried there. The Chamber of Commerce honored me for having done this—others resent me. Some days I resent myself. I resented myself to the extent that as soon as the St. Simons trilogy was written and my contracts fulfilled, I moved the locale of my next novels to St. Augustine, Florida. And for the next one, I will change locales again—to Savannah.

Yet, if my mail is any indication and if my own heart's desire counts, St. Simons will remain, to my readers and to me, a special place to be. My *home.* Part of the reason that is true is because in a particular way, the Island is, *in itself,* harmonious, orderly. A cosmos. With a life of its own. Novelists, perhaps, tend to anthropomorphize places and things. I even name my cars. It is, then, no surprise that I tend to give St. Simons a life of its own, a personality, a heart, a will to survive, in spite of high bridges and four-laned roads and bulldozers. There are times when I speak aloud to it: "You really are trying to *remain yourself,* aren't you, Island?"

5

And then I notice new, determined bright green vines struggling to cover the stump of a fallen tree, and I cheer.

The Indians called the St. Johns River, which flows north instead of south, We-la-ka: "The river with a way of its own." No one will ever shake my steadfast belief that St. Simons has a sheltering, seductive, singular, strong "way of its own."

At first I took for granted that everyone loved the Island for the same reasons I loved it—long-needled pines that catch the ever-changing light; resurrection ferns burgeoning along wide-branched oaks after a heavy rain; gold, gold leaves of twining bullis grapevines in autumn. I assumed everyone loved the Island history, its plantation families, its attraction not only to the military mind of General James Edward Oglethorpe, Georgia's founder, but to his heart as well. This is not necessarily true. These attractions, so fascinating to me, do not draw everyone who loves St. Simons. Even my dear friends, the oldtimers, didn't seem to know a lot about Island history. Few brightened with anything resembling proud recognition when Oglethorpe's name was mentioned. Many had never noticed the wonder of resurrection ferns, "risen from the dead" after a good rain. They all loved Island grapes, but few had thought about the (to me) exciting fact that God decorates His own trees at Christmas with those bright strands of yellow-leafed vines. No matter. *They loved the Island*, and their love was contagious.

New residents and visitors come for reasons which would certainly not attract me. Retirement, to rear their children here, golf, tennis, the beach, fishing. I have no children, never mean to retire, don't fish or play golf or tennis, much prefer James Gould's old plantation site as it once was: a breathtaking stand of tall trees and vines and palmetto. But St. Simons *is* a cosmos. With magnets enough for us all. It is

6